MEDICINE OF MY TIME

by

DONALD L. McNEIL, M.D.

**Interviews with Andras K. Kirchner and
William R. Maes
Edited by Andras K. Kirchner
Calgary 1989**

ISBN 0-88925-976-3

Published by
Maunders McNeil Foundation
522 Salem Avenue S.W.
Calgary, Alberta
T3C 2K6

First Printing, 1989

Printed and bound in Canada by
Friesen Printers
a Division of D.W. Friesen & Sons Ltd.
Altona, Manitoba R0G 0B0
Canada

INTRODUCTION

Dr. McNeil's Scottish ancestors settled in Ontario sometime in the mid 19th century and the family slowly drifted westward.

Dr. Donald L. McNeil was born in Estevan, Saskatchewan, educated in Winnipeg, Manitoba, and worked, with insignificant interruption, all his life in Calgary as a physician, specializing in internal medicine.

The story which we read on the following pages is his own life story, recorded first on tapes in a series of interviews, and transcribed to paper with my editorial care.

I met him first in 1983 during an official visit, when as a representative of the Alberta Medical Association, he was seeking a suitable place for the Association's archive.

I was captivated by his unusual humility which is so uncommon with men of his great stature, being President of the Alberta Medical Association, President of the Calgary Medical Society, and above all, an eminent physician.

The man radiates warmth which put me at ease and was the driving force throughout the interviews.

His life story typifies the fate of many Canadians of his generation: the good life of the twenties, the miseries of the depression years, and the war and its aftermath which is so significant in Canadian history. Dr. McNeil has a direct relationship with the University of Calgary. He organized and headed the University Student Health Services. It was as director of this service that he became advisor to the President of the University at the time and was instrumental in the establishment of the Medical Faculty.

Unfortunately, Dr. McNeil has not received any recognition for the important role he played in the formation of the Medical Faculty. This interview was intended to fill this hiatus and establish a memory for an excellent "Prairie doctor" whose dedication to his profession has been exemplary and should be quoted to future generations of medical students.

A. K. Kirchner

ONE

Kirchner: We may start the discussion with your recollection of childhood, your parents, their names, birthdates, and the way they lived.

McNeil: I am indeed honored that I am receiving this attention from you gentlemen. It is my sincere hope that the time you spend upon these visits will result in a story that will be worthy of your expectations. I have spent some time thinking about, and making notes for the response I will make to the questions I expect that you will ask.

To begin, then, my name is Donald Lauchlin McNeil. McNeil is a Scottish name as I'm sure you'll realize. The McNeil clan has a long history and the latter part of it is recorded, I understand. "Nial", the ancestor of MacNials of Barra, is the first who appears to occur in a charter, a document which is dated in the reign of King Robert the Bruce. A grandson of Nial settled in the Isle of Barra in the reign of King James, as seen in a charter dated 1427. The clan seems to have lived in Barra or Gigha or Colonsay, in islands of the Outer Hebrides of Scotland. Their history is quite fascinating to me as they were warlike and piratical. Their motto, "Vincere vel Mori", Victory or Death, might have brought about their extinction had they not been isolated to some degree from other warring tribes by their insular position. I first heard the designation of the "Black McNeils" from a Scot — the professor of gynecology — when he saw my name at the commencement of an oral examination, and possibly this relates to a somewhat different genealogy to other Scotch people. The coat of arms of the clan indicates a Norse origin and it is probable that they were ancestors of people who migrated from the Mediterranean and who occupied Ireland and later still eastern Scotland. Dad's father Lauchlin was born in Canada in Lanark County, Ontario. Lauchlin's wife Sarah Lamont was born in Scotland and remained on the Isle of Mull up until a short time before her marriage. Her mother and father had preceded her to Canada and were living on their farm nearby to the "grant land" of Lauchlin McNeil. I have heard that when leaving her home she did so with some considerable regret and is reputed to have said that she could not countenance not returning to Mull. She of course never did see Scotland again, being entirely preoccupied by the demands of her own enlarging family. Lauchlin obtained this grant land in Grey County, Ontario, and he at first, with Sarah his bride arriving about a year later, set about

1

to develop the farm and their home. The land was heavily treed and the work must have been tremendously hard. The need for heavy labor required for this and the general farm work was served well by the gradual acquisition of a large number of children. There were three boys and five girls.

Maes: About what time was this?

McNeil: This was in 1854 that they were married. Lauchlin made some preparatory work on the land a year before this. They were part of a Scottish community: hard working, God fearing, strictly religious people, usually of the Presbyterian persuasion.

Kirchner: You knew any one of them personally? The grandparents?

McNeil: No, I never did meet them. I learned of them from Dad. I did visit the community just before I graduated in medicine, when I accompanied Dad and my younger brother. By then it was an old, well developed area and I think would have been considered rich agricultural land. It was farmed intensively, and Ed and I were amazed by the small size of the farms as compared to those we were familiar with in the west. We learned later (not from Dad) of the brutally hard work that he did as a boy there. The attitude toward school was interesting; the children's involvement in education was entirely controlled by my grandfather. In the first year or two of Dad's schooling, when the work was all done in the fall, he was permitted to go to the schoolhouse, but with the first signs of spring he was told to bring home his slate and resume work on the farm. Two or three years later, he was told that his schooling was complete and he would now take his place as a man on the farm. There does not seem to have been much social life other than church which was attended several times a week. The future careers of the children would follow a set pattern again under the direction of their father. One son would remain on the family farm and the father would endeavor to obtain more land upon which future sons could begin their farm and home. The work on all the farms, as they increased in number, was planned and organized by the same person — the father. One of the boys, namely my father, ventured out and left Ontario. The options were rather limited; the boys were generally expected to carry on farm work. It is possible that one might have followed the highly regarded calling of the ministry and although such a career might tend to insure one for the life hereafter . . . in a Scotch home like this, I would suspect that the income of a clergyman might not provide sufficient security for the present life. A girl was expected to marry and the only other option might be that of a teacher. The Scotch were rigid and Dad's family were fiercely Scotch. I believe that he resented some of these influences and chose a much more tolerant personal path to follow for his future life. For example, I cannot remember that my father attended church, except on very rare occasions, after leaving his boyhood home. The environment in my mother's home was different and much more relaxed. Her father, Thomas Maunders, was born in Lincolnshire in England. He apparently was warm and endeared himself to the children, but may not have been as efficient as Dad's father. Her mother was Scotch and bore the maiden name of Mary Ann MacQuarrie. In contradistinction to the McNeil home where all worked hard, the mother (Mrs. Maunders) was not permitted to engage in housework. There was seemingly more gentleness in this family. Again there was a large number of children, four boys and four girls. Our mother, Annie, was quite close to the father, and whether this represented the Oedipus Complex or whether it indicated a less affectionate personality in her mother, I do not know. In mother's family, as the children matured, they followed a more classical career pattern. The oldest boy chose ranching and farming, probably supported initially by my grandfather. His life was more romantic and successful, living as he did in a number of places in North America. One boy became a physician and a medical missionary, but died rather prematurely at his home in Detroit. One followed the calling of the ministry and I believe that his "charges" were all in Western Canada. As the result of some dispute with regard to educational opportunities, the doctor and the minister were not on good terms and refused to see each other for the rest of their lives. One boy died in childhood. The girls all married and made their homes in various places across the continent. Mother's home was just a few miles from Dad's in the same county, close to the town of Brussels. When they had married

The McNeil's family home in Brussels, ca 1900. The house of the brothers' grandfather.

3

in 1900, they migrated to Western Canada and this step was a tremendous dislocation for our mother. I recall her telling me of the sadness she experienced on leaving home as she set out carrying the household effects which she had been given. It was with deep regret that she did not see her parents again.

Mother and Dad took up a "homestead" at Oakville, Manitoba, this area being part of the Portage Plains. The soil on these plains is a deep black loam, a remnant of the bottom of the ancient Lake Agassiz. It is reputed that this land has never experienced a crop failure. My mother and father had some early trials but not to the same degree as their parents. The land did not require, for example, the clearing of trees as was necessary in Ontario. They built their home, developed the farm, and survived very well. After ten years, they sold the established farm and I understand that they now considered themselves to be well off. They moved to southern Saskatchewan to a place called Estevan — a small town where a number of relatives and friends were now making their homes. Two of my uncles were the founders of the town. Dad, in his now rather affluent state, felt no urgency to go to work for the first time in his life. He looked at various endeavors that he might start, that is, when he wasn't enjoying the countryside while making housecalls with his crony, the local doctor.

Kirchner: Tell us, Dr. McNeil, more about your life in Estevan.

McNeil: It was in Estevan that the time was apparently right for the children to make their appearances. My older brother Maunders preceded me by four years and my younger brother Edmond followed two years later.

Of the various vocations that Dad tried in Estevan one was the owning and operating of a coal mine. This mine was really a shaft driven into the side of a hill and he called it, for some reason, "The Wollamalloo". This was seemingly the start of the family's interest in the coal and heating business. I have mused at times, would Dad's interest in coal stem from his dislike of cold — one of the antipathies that I share with him. I might mention that other relatives were active in the coal industry — our uncle, Mr. W. L. Hamilton, was one of the early mine operators producing lignite coal from the seams around nearby Bienfait. He was most notable, too, for his part in developing the rich bituminous coal fields in Crows Nest Pass and in Drumheller, Alberta. Another activity of Dad's that I remember was farm fencing, and as a small boy, having spent a few days with him whilst he was carrying this out, I can recall the process. The horse drawn wagon would slowly unreel the barbed wire as the posts were placed in the ground ahead of the unit. One might just reflect for a moment as to the millions of miles of barbed wire that was required to enclose farms on the prairies. Dad continued these several occupations during the ten years they were in Estevan. Mother was busy then raising her family, attending to church and missionary work, helping younger wives with their cooking and sewing, etc. Politics was always a major challenge and a life long interest to her. She was an active supporter of the Women's Christian Temperance Union and I recall that she was joined in this by our saintly aunt. Aunt Jessie's husband (my uncle) was a founder of the town, had wide business interests, and perhaps most notable, was the town magistrate. His heavy indulgence in alcohol remained a secret till his late life when another illness exposed his weakness.

There were some firsts for us in Estevan such as our first car. I remember Dad installing a "self starter" in our Hupmobile. Maunders and I commenced school in this small town. I do not remember very much of school there, but one incident does stand out in my mind. The teacher felt that it was incumbent upon her to call the school doctor (our old family friend and family physician) with regard to me. She believed that she could perceive something in my eyes which had an ominous portent for me. I was said to have big brown eyes and somehow this must have influenced her to think that I must be guilty of an unspeakable practice. Also, at age four, I can remember Armistice Day of 1918 when the town burned an effigy of the German Kaiser. This must have occurred in a thousand towns and villages in the world that night. Bordering the town is a great valley where the soil is a deep red and as I remember grew very little. No one lived there and the place was made more eerie by the presence of an Indian grave or two. As I thought about it at some later time, I wondered just what this land might be good for — "perhaps they would find oil there some day". This area became a moderate producer of "Black Gold". There was much to make life happy for the whole family in Estevan. When we moved from Estevan it was to proceed to Winnipeg.

TWO

McNeil: We left Estevan in November 1920 at a time when the first signs of winter and snow were evident. We had a distance to travel of about 300 miles and the journey was made in an open touring car, a gray "Dort". This was a popular car of the time, long since out of production. I saw such a car restored on a visit to Ontario a few years back. The trip to Winnipeg is still vivid in my mind. We were wrapped in blankets and an attempt was made to keep our feet warm by starting each day with bricks heated in the oven in the place we stayed the night before. The narrow tires, the snow, the uncertain road, and a slight hill made forward motion often impossible. While I think of it, gentlemen, those undeveloped mud roads were difficult in the winter, but on a wet summer day they were almost impossible to navigate. The car would slither on the ungravelled road from one ditch to the other.

Mother was a major influence in our move to Winnipeg. She was determined that her boys would have the opportunity of a university education, and moving to this city where there was a university, would facilitate her plans. Our move brought us to a home situated in the center of the city not far from where the Eaton's store is located. We lived in that house for the next ten years. Winnipeg, situated at the junction of the Red and Assiniboine River, was then considered the "gateway to the west". It contained, I believe, the largest railway yards in the world and these lines fanned out to all of Western Canada. The grain exchanges in Winnipeg and Chicago controlled most of the grain business in North America. Here too were the large warehouses and offices of the great wholesale and distribution companies, one of which was of course the T. Eaton Company, with its mail order facilities.

The city contained a great cross section of people; the wealthy grain and wholesale merchants with their large homes lived on the south side of the city; the middle class, who served business, lived on the north and west sides of the city. There were large ethnic groups — Chinese, Central and Eastern European people, Jewish, Italian, Indian and Metis. Of course, Winnipeg is adjacent to the large, entirely French city of St. Boniface. Many of these ethnic groups were immigrants brought to Canada probably as a result of unfavorable conditions in their homeland, but also because of the bright prospects of Western Canada as portrayed by the C.P.R. These people often suffered greatly

6

in this climate. It was in north Winnipeg that the C.C.F. party, later to become the New Democratic Party, was born. Mr. Woodsworth, the founder, while attempting to alleviate their needs through his "mission", saw the suffering first hand. The great Winnipeg Strike, involving war veterans with loss of life, had occurred only a year before our arrival. Social functions were common and the more lavish events were staged in the large railway hotels. Private clubs existed for the well to do. Theater was available and visiting artists from England and the U.S.A. commonly performed. It is interesting to note that the city fostered the development of important visual arts. This came about in the following way — Eaton's mail order house required large amount of graphic copy for their catalogues and this work was tendered out to the printing and graphic trades. The work was largely handled by one company, namely Brigdens, a firm my brother Maunders remembers well. This work attracted artistic talent. The offices were larger in Winnipeg than even the firm's main office in Toronto. Such Group of Seven artists as Tom Thompson were at one time employed there. Brigdens paid menial wages and supplied poor working conditions, but the plant became aptly termed a "hot house of Canadian art". Many Western Canadian artists originated or were associated with Brigdens — men such as Mr. W. J. Phillips, Nicholas Grandmaison, Charles Comfort, and Eric Bergman are but a few.

Our home on Carlton Street (the Carlton Trail famous in the story of the Riel Rebellion) was very close to the school we attended. I can

The McNeil brothers' family home; 182 Carlton Street, Winnipeg, ca 1920.

remember taking out a large school window with a ball batted from our backyard. I can still see the teacher poking her head through the broken pane. This backyard was the center for our "gang", where we played sports, planned the next fishing outing, or a visit to the swimming hole, and held our meetings with our resolutions often "sealed in blood". It was the place where we repaired our bikes, chopped wood, or wielded the carpet beater each spring. There were no vacuum cleaners and when that carpet was struck as it hung on the clothes line you were enveloped in a cloud of dust. Living that close to the school, my tardy nature was particularly exasperating to the teachers when I would frequently arrive late for school. My closest friend, who still remains in my high esteem, was obliged to leave school when he was in grade five and go to work because of his family's economic state. He has now a deserved high reputation as a citizen of this country in peace and war. This was Borden Galloway, (Borden, the name taken from the wartime Canadian prime minister, Sir Robert Borden). "Bordy" and I shared many experiences; as boys we roamed far and wide around that city looking for adventure or a new swimming hole; on one bitterly cold day in the center of the Assiniboine River, near its junction with the Red River, I broke through the ice. Holding onto the edge of the hole, I was pulled out by Bordy only to break through again a few feet away from the first hole. After I was pulled out the second time we made for his house at least a mile away. It took some time to dry my clothes before going home where the event was never mentioned. If we could just get out, say on a Saturday morning, without having the day ruined by some household chore, we kept our ventures pretty well to ourselves. Our values were very much like those of Mark Twain's Tom Sawyer. We attended elementary and junior high schools here in this neighborhood. In these classes I still believe that I obtained some early appreciation of English Literature notwithstanding the tiresome ordeal of memorizing lines of Shakespeare from perhaps Macbeth, or a poem of Tennyson's. We were required to learn two languages. I can remember the principal talking to me when he recommended that I stop the French lessons as he said that I seemed to manage the Latin all right, but that I was quite hopeless in learning French. Unfortunately, my inability or laziness to learn this language was a disadvantage which I regretted many times. The syntax, though, remained forever backwards to me. I later was able to learn German and Latin without any particular difficulty. We studied history quite diligently, but this was English history and Eastern Canadian history. We memorized the travels of Champlain, for example, but knew little of the great Western explorers, such as Thompson or La Verendrye. Discipline was quite positive − one's hands would be quite swollen for a number of days after experiencing the "strap". We received manual training where one learned to use the basic carpentry tools.

We would bring our wooden bookends, or whatever, home with their woodcarving showing the results of frequent slips of the chisel. I can remember that the manual training teacher could and did use the strap too. Such an occurrence was never mentioned at home, as the rule was that the same punishment would be repeated there. Mother would have the three boys shining and clean in our best clothes (as small boys — red velvet with a broad stiff collar) in our pew at Knox Church, each Sunday morning and at Sunday School in the afternoon. Dad was notable by his absence at church as I have alluded to previously. I have the impression that he did not have a high regard for ministers in general. We were required to say our prayers every night. We each possessed a Bible, a present received on some occasion such as our birthday or Christmas, and Mother expected us to read it frequently. I remember receiving John Bunyan's The Pilgrim's Progress, again as a present, and can recall descriptions of the "Slough of Despond" or the pilgrim learning the inadequacies of the law and the legal system in relation to the Christian faith.

We moved from Carlton Street out to the west end of the city in 1930. This home was on the edge of the city and I have seen snow higher than the first storey of the house as it blew in from the prairies. I attended Gordon Bell High School, named after the father of one of my later medical teachers. I left school for one year at this time, as I had become tired of formal education. I obtained a job at a local drug store and my plan was to complete my matriculation with night courses and then apprentice as a pharmacist. I learned something of pharmacy but after a year I approached Dad asking if I might return to school. I fortunately realized what I was losing in not continuing school. He agreed rather resignedly and I returned to my studies with quite a different attitude to that of the previous year. As time passed and my educational resolve became more evident, Dad became my staunch supporter.

At this time, gentlemen, I would like to tell you something of the family business. When we came to Winnipeg Dad started a fuel yard called H. J. McNeil. The offices and the large coal sheds were placed on land situated on a railway siding. The coal arrived from the mines in boxcars containing from forty to sixty tons and was unloaded by hand with wheelbarrows moving over trestles. The wood arrived in box cars had been cut in four foot lengths, and after unloading it was necessary to cut these in stove lengths. I can remember as a small boy having tinkered with the balance of the large scale used to weigh loads, and this resulted in Dad being publicly reported and fined, because when a load was checked at a city scale it was found to be short in weight. In the earliest years the coal was moved by horse-drawn sleighs, but this method of delivery gradually changed and was replaced by trucks. The three boys wanted to work at the "yard" as we became

The H. J. McNeil Coal Coke & Wood Business in Winnipeg, ca 1925. At the right of the automobile is Hector McNeil and at the left Ed.

big enough to do some labor. I don't think we were paid anything for our work, unless it was a promise that we receive a little money to enable us to exchange family Christmas presents. I would work later on at the coal yard, not only up until the university session started in the fall, but also on weekends and holidays. Whilst things were very busy during the cold winter the coal yard was a dormant place in the summer. Dad would have us occupy our time by repairing equipment or working on certain buildings which he managed. We had the opportunity to do some farm work on a farm he had bought for speculation, and "stooking grain" was, I found, to be distinctly hard work. I remember that the farm was not a profitable speculation having been held too long into the depression years.

To return to school experiences, I entered Kelvin Technical High School. This was a large school and was technical in that they taught certain trades as well. I did, for example, learn pattern making, metal casting, wood turning, and draughting.

There were many good influences at Kelvin. Sports were encouraged and I remember how impressed I was when I heard an academic teacher goad me on personally when I was competing in the only athletic event that I ever attempted. Kelvin regularly posted the largest number of points in the annual field day for all the Winnipeg high schools. I made notes with regard to some of the teachers. The principal was Mr. Hodgson, who we regarded as a good friend. You could visit him if you wished and with an enrollment at Kelvin of over a thousand, he remains as one of my most admired people. A teacher by the name of Padwig taught us Latin. He would teach us the primary composition and the grammar construction for only a very few hours of the year. We had to make some effort to learn vocabulary. The rest of the session he would spend with us in talking about all kinds of other subjects. We would spend some time on Latin "authors" such as the literature was called. Virgil and Homer and the orations of Cicero were the ones I recall reading.

Kirchner: You mean in English translation or in Latin?

McNeil: In Latin and attempting from our knowledge of the language to understand the passage. I recall with admiration the chemistry teacher we had, a Mr. Wharton, who gave us a firm, basic grounding in the subject. University chemistry was not difficult for me after that. He had been a major league baseball umpire, prior to teaching, and with his loud booming voice he had no trouble in commanding attention. Mr. Jewitt, the math teacher, had a strong influence upon many Winnipeg high school students. He has been honored many times in later years. He was forceful, but one realized that he regarded your process of thought rather than the answer, and his appreciation of this in you did something for your self esteem.

Kirchner: Before we go any further, I would like you to provide us with your father's and your mother's names.

McNeil: Dad's name was Hector James McNeil. His father's name

Hector J. McNeil, 1943.

11

Mrs. Annie McNeil, ca 1938.

was Lauchlin, and my second name is taken from the grandfather. Mother's name was Annie Maunders — I don't remember her having a second name.

Kirchner: Both families were orientated towards professional work rather than farming?

McNeil: I would think that my grandparents felt that farming was the basis for the other things. The church was also most important. I would think that the profession of a physician or a teacher was necessary but not as fundamental as the work of the soil.

Kirchner: Can you tell us something about your brothers?

McNeil: Maunders, my older brother, was given Mother's surname as his first name. He has remained in the family business. When gas and oil became available in Winnipeg, the merchandizing of coal became impractical. He started the heating and air conditioning business and the company has grown and prospered in Western Canada. We had all worked in the coal business; we drove trucks and we shovelled coal. I don't think that I was ever a very great workman. Edmond, our younger brother, joined Maun in the new heating and air conditioning enterprise after he returned from overseas and war service. Ed is retired from the business now. Maunders still carries on the management of the company and has associated with him Ed's two sons, James and David McNeil. This is quite a large wholesale type business with branches across Western Canada from Winnipeg to Calgary in all of the major cities. Maunders remains active and successful — still with the major burden of the large business. He applies the same old rules my father did to business — he operates with great dedication, courage, vision, and care in all his dealings. I think this must provide the explanation for the success that the enterprise has enjoyed. Ed had been the vice president of the company, providing his particular "dedication" up until the time he chose to retire.

THREE

Kirchner: When were you born?

McNeil: I was born on the fifth of May, 1914. Just a few months before the outbreak of the first war.

Kirchner: Now, as you were the middle boy, what was the quality of the relationship with your brothers?

McNeil: I always felt closer to my younger brother Ed, but Maun was, I'm sure, rather the ideal to both of us. Maun has always had, and continues to assume, a responsibility as the senior member of the family — rather as though in trust for Dad.

Kirchner: We have been talking in a time frame of 1914 on. Would you tell us something about your recollections of the 1920's and the 1930's?

McNeil: I remember a little bit of the 20's. I was entering my teens then and have some appreciation of the "roaring 20's". I know what the cars looked like, how people dressed, the Charleston, prohibition, the speakeasies, and the gangsters in nearby Chicago. I can remember the night in 1929 when the stock market fell in New York. I was working at the drug store and realized that something terribly exciting had happened. The great depression was to follow but that, with all its suffering, could not be predicted then by anyone. It was by means of an "Extra" paper that one learned of some important event. We were using radio but this was not available in many homes. Maun had rigged up a "crystal set" but only one person could listen with earphones. For those few who could afford one of the larger more complex sets — these families and friends might stay up late into the night to listen for the "call letters" and search for the more distant stations. We could see a great Western silent movie (accompanied by suitable thrilling piano music) for 10 cents–an amount we often did not have. All three boys had paper routes for several years. These were delivered daily and twice on Saturdays. The routes made us independent financially and we now purchased our own clothes of the style and fashion we liked. While delivering my papers one Saturday and trying to direct a rather dull boy, who had been helping me, I was struck by a car. I had amnesia and acted quite strangely for the next twenty four hours. I was put to bed and when I seemed all right the next day, it was not considered necessary to call the doctor. That one took the step to call the doctor was a decision not taken lightly. Doctor Scarlett wrote an interesting paper at one time describing the seriousness felt in a neighborhood when the word went out that some household had "called the doctor". It was at a war medicine course in London as I listened to a lecturer talking on head injuries and learning of the commonest sequelae of this trauma (loss of the sense of smell) that I related that paper route accident to my total loss of the ability to smell.

The depression was more than just in business — it was a depression of the spirit; indeed you could feel it everywhere. I certainly saw it in my Dad, who had been, until now, fairly successful. He had become involved in a number of business ventures as had so many others. He, like so many others, experienced great distress when the effects of the "crash" were felt. There has been much written about these years and I saw something of the hardships as told in these accounts. The coal business, however, carried on through all the bad years and seemed affluent at least during the winter time. Large amounts of money were handled then as the cost of importing and freight were significant. The profits perhaps weren't that great, but it seemed like we had a lot of money, and were better off during the winter. With the cold weather (Winnipeg can get cold!) our spirits picked up, but in hot, mid-summer they would fall. There was little or no opportunity to find work of any other kind. We spent our time repairing, painting, and fixing up the equipment around the coal yard. Dad did find some other work in connection with some real estate and buildings which he supervised for a wealthy American. In the very early stage of the depression this American business magnate suddenly called upon Dad for a large sum of money. This caused great consternation to my father. It was not that the equity did not exist but funds were tied up in newly purchased buildings and probably in some of Dad's ventures. This business relationship was founded upon great trust between Dad and this man. I was impressed, and have remained so, that when this request for money came Dad's almost immediate response was to visit Mr. Lee in Detroit. I learned then something of the shocking effects felt when property values and assets dropped so greatly.

Kirchner: With regard to your career it would be interesting to know who influenced you. Who was the decision maker in the family?

McNeil: Well, Mr. Kirchner and Mr. Maes, I have noted your question and have given my response considerable thought. Of course, there was the influence and support of the family. To describe this background I wish to tell you something about the personalities of the family. Mother and Dad possessed much the same qualities of character. They believed in hard work, diligence, the importance of saving, honesty, conformity to the "golden rule", humility, and modesty. As an example of personal modesty, Mother told me that she refused pelvic examination when giving birth to her first child.

15

Mother maintained deep religious convictions all her life. Dad did not demonstrate similar attitudes toward religious belief. Mother was gregarious in all her activities, be it the church, her home, a game such as cards (never on Sunday), in her ambitions for her boys, and especially in her politics (conservatism). She was ready to round up a conservative rally wherever she might be. She loved to joust with a liberal (with no acrimony). She lived to the ripe age of 104 and we sometimes thought her passing was postponed to see Trudeau gone. Dad had these qualities of character, as I have already stated, but lived a quiet, unselfish, and

Mrs. Annie McNeil with her sons Ed, Don and Maun at her 100th birthday, 1975.

sincere life. He was not impressed with higher education in itself. He could not comprehend the value of humanities or an arts degree for an individual to earn a living. He did, however, quietly support me in my decision and choice to follow the study of medicine. He could understand that profession, and I realized he followed my career with some pride. For example, although university fees were small in comparison to present standards, they were still formidable and he could somehow find these funds in spite of the terrible depression. Once, while I was in the midst of studying and attempting to learn all the vast knowledge of medicine, he placed on my desk a copy he had framed of the complete poem by Kipling, "If". You will remember it I'm sure:
    "If you think you are beaten you are,
    If you think you dare not you don't,

If you would like to win but think you can't
It is almost a cinch you won't . . .''

I wish now, as I'm sure many others have done, that I could have appreciated more of those basic values that Mother and Dad upheld. I do remember Dad as standing quietly aside while all the family watched me board a train for overseas on a cold winter train platform in Winnipeg — the last time I saw him.

Maunders possesses the aggressive tenacious personality of Mother which has influenced his successful career in business, his community, and charitable endeavors. He and my younger brother Ed sacrificed much during those depression years to advance my progress. Ed has always been a loyal, hard working, good citizen, family man, Mason and Shriner. Ed was a great support to Mother and Father in their later years. Maunders, however, has never forsaken his responsibility as the eldest son. I believe he considers it a trust to support, in every way, the continued close association of the boys in honor of our father and mother. Maunders, on a festive occasion, was once described (perhaps a little irreverently) as the ''God-father''.

Other influences on my career that I can think of are: I was a little bit of a dreamer, and reading books like *Microbe Hunters* by Paul de Kruif and *Arrowsmith* by Sinclair Lewis fueled a very sincere desire in me to follow medicine as a career. I suppose I was always somewhat of a romanticist. As a boy, I did have, perhaps unusual for a prairie lad, an early desire to go to ''sea'' . No one in the family could really understand this. I had in mind the merchant navy or the navy and this would have been the Royal Navy as Canada didn't seem to have much of a navy then. I was an active member of the Sea Cadets. I had written letters to at least one of the great training ships in England. Such a whim could not be countenanced by my more practical parents. This desire gradually passed, but perhaps the dream was partially fulfilled later and should there be time perhaps I can tell you of the boat I built.

Kirchner: Sports and athletic interests are associated with almost every occupation nowadays. Would you tell me please what your inclinations might have been as a young man?

McNeil: My interest in sports was minimal; I earned one pennant at Kelvin where athletics were encouraged. I have always enjoyed aquatic sports and particularly boating. I did build the family boat myself, a fairly large one with a cabin. This was built at a time when I was most active in practice and the boat remains in operation some 25 years later. Maun was quite a good athlete in track and field, etc. When reflecting upon your questions to the things that might have influenced me to follow the calling of medicine, I remembered rather poignantly an event in first year medicine which I would like to relate to you. The Dean of Medicine at Manitoba at that time was a psychiatrist. We all knew that at some time during the year we would be summoned to his office and would be expected to respond to a specific question — why did you choose to become a doctor? To us, all rather humble students, we looked upon Doctor Mather awesomely. For weeks beforehand, we would think about this; some stated that they would give an altruistic explanation proclaiming lofty motives as their reason. Others professed that they would become more practical and said they would confess monetary and social rewards. The question was appropriate I think for a psychiatrist. Dr. Mather accepted my explanation; and I remember that he seemed pleased when part of my reply related to Dad's old crony, Dr. Henry, the family doctor in Estevan.

FOUR

Kirchner: Would you tell us where and when you attended university and something about the nature of your courses?

McNeil: I began pre-medicine in Winnipeg at the United College. This was then a church college in 1932. You said that you would be interested in the costs of my education. I remember that my total fees, other than books, for the first year was $128.00 and the second year was about $160.00. For the final years in medicine the fees reached close to $300.00. I look back kindly upon the bursar who was most tolerant in those years with regard to installment payments. United College was a little bit "old world"; the professors wore gowns and there was chapel each morning. I rather enjoyed chapel, where the address was commonly delivered by the Dean or the Chaplain and sometimes was given by some notable visitor. I remember one such visitor, a Canadian author with the pen name of Ralph Connor – whose books I had read previously, *The Man from Glengarry* and *Sowing Seeds in Danny*.

I had two years of German in pre-med and that, along with my high school Latin, fulfilled the requirements of two languages for medicine. We attempted some German literature including prose and some scientific papers. The higher mathematics required was obtained by completing a full year of analytical geometry. We continued chemistry with classroom and laboratory work, taking inorganic chemistry the first year and organic chemistry the second. The first lecture in organic chemistry is still vivid in my mind. Colonel Armes, the professor, leaned on his cane, obviously an amputee of the previous war. I could understand his reaction to students who were inclined at that time to support positions such as "I will not bear arms". As I have said, chemistry was rather easy having had an excellent high school background in that subject. The course work was completed at two institutions, the first the United College and the second the University of Manitoba. We received two years of Humanities by means of a very long course in English spanning literature from Chaucer to contemporary authors. I appreciated this study and remember one thoughtful student stating that this course would constitute his religion. I find it difficult to believe when I learn that students, perhaps more often in American universities, are not required to have humanity

19

credits. The subject of Botany was provided by a department headed by a notable Dr. Buller. Dr. Wardle, the head of the department of Zoology, stimulated our interest in Biology.

The downtown branch of the University of Manitoba, which I attended, was situated close to the Manitoba Legislature buildings and the law courts. I spent some worthwhile hours attending court and watching the proceedings — mostly of criminal trials.

Maes: How large would the classes have been at that time? Were they quite large or would the freshman class have been a very large class?

McNeil: No, there wouldn't be more than about 40 to 50 people.

Kirchner: How would you evaluate your teachers and the University at that time?

McNeil: Although we probably did not appreciate our teachers to the degree that we should have, I firmly believe that teachers such as Drs. Buller, Wardle, Armes, etc. were superior. The University was in poor financial straits for it was the middle of the depression. The institution had lost its entire endowment fund as a result of fraud. The treasurer had dipped into these funds, to support his trading ventures on the Winnipeg Grain Exchange, and managed to deplete all of the monies. The campus downtown was not attractive, and it was in the process of being phased out, and moved to the beautiful site of the old Manitoba Agricultural College at Fort Garry. The facilities did not match the quality of the teaching!

Kirchner: Would you deal with your formal courses in medicine?

McNeil: Having completed my two years, I now made application to the Faculty of Medicine. It was required that you have a clear passing from the pre-medical course. There was no interview or selection committee; your application was considered on the basis of your academic results plus the documentation which one completed. There was a little scandal some years later when the Jewish community called for a review of this admission procedure as they believed that they were being treated with discrimination. There was a large population of Jewish people in Winnipeg, as I have already said — probably a third of our class would have been of that religious faith. The Jewish doctors regularly became renowned as teachers and practitioners.

I wasn't at all sure that I could raise the tuition money to enter medical school even though I had been accepted. I visited the college in the summer and advised them that I would not be able to proceed with studies because of economic reasons. I could not see how I might raise about $250.00 for the tuition. Dear old Dad thought differently and somehow was able to see that my plans were not interrupted. I entered medical school in the fall of 1934 with the prospect of a long five year course ahead of me. Four years were spent at the University and the fifth year in a hospital as a junior intern. In our first year at the school we did do a tremendous amount of anatomy. It amounted to ten, twelve, or more hours per week. I think we spent more hours than this in the anatomy department because we would collect there like students might to a "common room". We discussed anything and everything over our cadaver or "stiff".

Kirchner: This was macroscopic anatomy?

McNeil: Yes, macroscopic anatomy – histology or microscopic anatomy was a separate course.

We enjoyed anatomy and greatly respected the professors. The demonstrators were practicing physicians and from them we had our first introduction to actual medicine. Some of their stories were most interesting but I know I must not take the time to relate them. Four first year men worked on the upper half of the cadaver whilst four second year men worked on the lower half. Anatomy was a two year course and our dissection was done with greatest of care; no surgeon dissected more carefully. Our exposure of structures was meticulous and it was a real disaster if some foolish person made a careless move and destroyed something that prevented detailed examination of a part. I remember that our examinations were most serious and in oral tests various tricks were used such as to put a vertebra in a closed bag and you were expected to palpate the bag and announce where that vertebra came from — what part of the spine. It wasn't too difficult, but you were expected to define the level quite accurately, such as L4 or C2. I look back nostalgically upon our anatomy professor, Dr. Ingster.

Physiology was a very intense, serious course with lectures and long hours spent in the laboratories. Our work was monitored very carefully. I don't know whether graphs are still in use. These graphs rotated on two drums; the stylus would record the vital changes resulting from your application of some drug or chemical to your live animal. We felt some tension in the presence of faculty members; in particular, the stony countenance of Dr. Moorhouse, the head of the department. We carried out our work on live animals, first with frogs and later with dogs, cats and turtles. I did tire from endless experiments with frogs as we applied chemicals and observed the responses upon muscle contraction. Where anatomy was considered by us an introduction to medicine in general, physiology gave us our first taste of surgery, at least in the laboratory experience. It was most important to learn the function of the vagus nerve and we believed that if you learned this properly the knowledge of pharmacology and therapeutics rested on a firm basis. The vagus nerve (the parasympathetic nervous system) and the understanding of its function, I believe, is still a fundamental requirement for medicine.

We spent long hours at biochemistry. A Professor Cameron was our teacher and wrote our textbook which I still have. I may still occasionally refer to it, but it was certainly worked over by me in those years.

Kirchner: And bacteriology started in the second year?

McNeil: Yes, bacteriology started then. We also carried on with our anatomy, physiology, biochemistry, and we took pharmacology, and materia medica. The latter course would now seem strange to the present day medical student. It dealt with, as you know, therapeutic substances commonly in their basic or original states. We learned our bacteriology through lectures and laboratory work. We were required to identify and classify bacteria and micro-organisms by their microscopic appearance, culture characteristics, staining properties, etc. These labs were adjacent to the large provincial laboratories, where Wassermans were done, and I recall viewing those large trays of test tubes, where the clear supernatant fluid indicated a Four Plus test; a common observation on any morning. Now we, most importantly, commenced our studies in pathology.

Kirchner: These were mostly lectures?

McNeil: Yes, lectures in pathology given by the famous Dr. William Boyd. Dr. Boyd, through the textbook he wrote and which was used widely in North America and elsewhere, had a great influence on medical teaching. He died only a few years ago. He was one of three remarkable physicians who came from Scotland to Winnipeg about the same time. The three Scotsmen were namely Drs. William Boyd, Grant and Gibson. Dr. Grant, who wrote a textbook of anatomy (which I believe is still in use), moved to Toronto as head of the department before I came. Dr. Gibson, a notable orthopedic surgeon in Winnipeg, is possibly still known for an exposure of the hip joint which he developed.

These three doctors made quite an impact on medicine, at least on this continent. Dr. Boyd was not a trained pathologist when he came to Manitoba. He had apparently replied to an advertisment of the University of Manitoba who was seeking qualified faculty for the medical school. The advertisement was ambiguous, and failed to indicate that the applicants' qualifications must be specifically in pathology. He did not venture that his qualifications were not in pathology. That story is remarkable in that Dr. Boyd became a world renowned authority in this area of medicine. We used the book *General Pathology* mostly. There was a surgical pathology and also a pathology of internal medicine written by him. We were required to know the book in its entirety. Two or three students would be designated for each class, to be familiar with every reference in the bibliography of the text pertaining to the subject for the day. I well remember those lectures as he had some unique methods of teaching. To remember something he would use association. For example, a Dr. Rich was well known in the field of virology then. He told us that whenever he thought of Rich, he recalled an evening in a hotel room where Dr. Rich demonstrated his ability to drink out of the opposite side of the glass. When I heard of Dr. Rich in later years, I too, thought of this association. The pathology laboratory was unique. The specimens were placed on a piece of plate glass, with a large sealed watch glass over that, so you saw the specimen clearly. It was not contained in an old bottle as was the usual custom. The specimen in its container lay on an inclined table top for the student's benefit. You read not only the pathological report of that particular piece of tissue, but there was also the medical history of the owner of that specimen. Pathology became a living process rather than a "dead" subject, and that has been Dr. Boyd's contribution to pathology. The pathology course was very intense and we certainly learned the subject. I obtained 99% on an exam on one occasion, but failed another term exam — the only time I ever failed anything at university. I can remember that exam very well; one question was as follows: "What happens to the myocardium, (the heart) when you have a coronary occlusion?" I remember sitting down and wondering, "what could happen to the heart?" Well, the tissue dies in the area of the infarct and the intra cardiac pressure acts upon the area. I wrote down: "The heart ruptures". That, and one or two other mistakes, and I received less than 50%. I remember him telling us, "the heart does not rupture. You die from various other things, but the heart will rupture in only .5% or some such small fraction." Boyd had a large influence upon us. He was away often because other demands were made upon his time. His associates, Dr. Sara Meltzer and Dr. Dan Nicholson, were excellent pathologists and teachers.

Kirchner: Dr. Nicholson — well known, his name!

McNeil: I'm glad I mentioned it, he did write a book on laboratory medicine. We had a full course in this subject. We were required to have our own microscopes throughout our student years. We possessed other laboratory equipment so that we could do our own blood counts, etc. We learned to do most laboratory procedures, and I recall for some reason the Folin Woo method of measuring blood sugars.

FIVE

Kirchner: What kind of a relationship did the students have with their professors?

McNeil: We were, generally speaking, distanced from senior faculty. We would talk to another student, to a senior student or to a friendly laboratory demonstrator if we were troubled, but to seek out the head of the department would be a rarity. The senior professors, such as Dr. Boyd, would have appreciated it, and openly invited dialogue. I remember Dr. Boyd's invitation to do just this, but there was an invisible wall. I distinctly recall going to Dr. Moorehouse once. I couldn't understand "decerebrate rigidity" and with trepidation I ventured into his office. The pleasant reception I received was a surprise and I did learn the physiological explanation of the process. Some of the junior professors were rather arrogant: for example, in biochemistry we were required to do a quantitative measurement of calcium in the blood. The exercise was a straightforward one; everyone in the class received 100% on their results, but I managed only 2%. I went to see the second in command of the department, a Dr. White who supervised the laboratory work, and asked him if he could give me any idea of what I'd done wrong. His reply was, "I can't tell you anything; you'd just better go and do your work." It was in our second year that we first saw a patient. We had a course in physical diagnosis and this was of great interest to us. We were taught in this class the process of physical examination — the proper method of performing a medical examination including the neurological exam.

Kirchner: Was this at the bedside?

McNeil: Yes, this was at the bedside. We were formed in groups of about ten students. We continued in these same groups through the next three years. We appeared at the hospital at a certain specified hour for the purpose of attending a clinic. These clinics were supervised by a clinician, a physician, and were convened on the hospital ward or in the outdoor department of the hospital. A careful history and physical examination was stressed even more then than I believe it is now. I recall the first day we considered the examination of the abdomen. One of my classmates, a good student was asked, "What can you palpate in the abdomen?" He did not know so he recited a list of every organ that is present in the abdomen. The proper reply

24

should have been "You can feel nothing in the abdomen normally." The student, a capable orthopedic surgeon in Vancouver now, would never forget it either because of the humility he was made to feel that day.

Maes: Dr. McNeil, would that have been a course that ran the length of the year?

McNeil: Yes, it ran the whole year. It might have been 1 or 2 hours a week. We felt very important — we now had a stethoscope in our pockets! We commonly travelled home on the street cars and when, in first year, we might have human bones sticking out of our pockets, we now had stethoscopes hanging in partial view.

Kirchner: Medical students were considered as prestigious people in your time?

McNeil: Yes. We smelled of the labs; first of the anatomy labs where formaldehyde was used, then later of ether. Someone standing next to us would be aware, and possibly recognize our occupation. The next two years, the third and fourth, constituted our clinical years. We continued pathology in third year but now we commenced our lectures in Medicine, Surgery, Gynecology and Obstetrics, which were interspersed with clinics held in various hospitals. The outdoor services provided a wealth of clinical material. We saw, first-hand, diseases in all their stages, fascinating thing such as a G.P.I. (General Paralysis of the Insane) and any of the stages of syphilis quite regularly. I remember seeing the "King of the Bums". These so called "Bums" were people who rode the rails (freight cars) in those years. This one man called himself the "King of the Bums"; to illustrate this he had numerous medals (bottle tops) all over his clothes, and his Wasserman was not unexpectedly four plus. He would have been shipped off to a mental hospital to have received Tryparsamide, one of the arsenicals used for neurosyphilis, or he would be given the disease malaria. We gave malaria to such patients for the purpose of producing high fevers. The symptoms often ameliorated with such treatment and a psychosis might clear. We saw large aortic aneurysms bulging out of chests and we put flags on them to demonstrate the movement of the tumor.

The teaching was given by qualified specialists in their field. There was some subspecialty training given, for example, in E.N.T. Ophthalmology, Orthopedics, and even Dentistry (I removed quite a number of teeth), but generally the emphasis was on the basic divisions of medicine. In class you would spend several sessions upon the subject of peptic ulcers with a gastroenterologist. We were well aware of the benefits of a Sippy diet.

There was no General Practice teaching and similary no allotted time to spend in this area. I know that special training may be advocated now, but I cannot accept that the basic learning material should differ. Teaching by those who are particularly qualified should be available to all students. Our course in Public Health was instructive with such exercises as the visit to learn something of the operation of a brewery, or an abattoir to observe the process of killing cattle, disease recognition, and preparation of meat. The class in Jurisprudence was most interesting, with the fascination of forensic medicine, the compulsory attendance at inquests, familiarization with the courts, and even the inside of a jail.

Our patients in the outdoor units and in the hospital were what were termed "staff patients". These were charity patients who paid little or nothing for their medical care. They were under the supervison of the university staff but actual procedures might be carried out by residents. I believe the attention they received was excellent and surely often better than they might have obtained privately. Such a designation would be unacceptable now — but in our "advanced" society of today, freedoms too have been lost. The patients presently in a teaching hospital do not have the right to free choice of his or her doctor, and little voice in their own disposition. In Obstetrics we were required to attend some thirty births in the undergraduate years. Our same small group of students would receive a summons by phone, and would, by prior arrangement, travel in one or two cars to any hospital at any time of day or night for this purpose.

Kirchner: This was a norm? An obligatory norm?

McNeil: Yes, obligatory. I remember that I became quite competent and usually very accurate in my observation by external obstetrical examination. Later on, when as an intern, I advised my preceptor that the presentation of a particular baby was to be a "breech". Following a pelvic exam that he carried out, he assured me that I was wrong, and further, that as I seemed incompetent in such a basic observation, I should arrange that the resident carry out this delivery. That baby delivered as a "breech".

Kirchner: So that, in fact, direct contact with patients went on from the 2nd year, most likely intensified later?

McNeil: Yes, it increased greatly. Our oral and practical examinations were carried out with patients.

Kirchner: That's exactly what I wanted to ask you. Tell us something about the way examinations were carried out.

McNeil: The final written examinations were invigilated in large rooms, where there would be several hundred students from all faculties. The mid-term examinations were carried out at the medical school, but end of the year examinations took place at the university situated some distance from our medical college. The preparations we made for examination were intensive. I know my friends and I might stay up until 3:00 or 4:00 in the morning for days preceding the tests. It truly meant "burning the midnight oil"! The exams followed one after the other over a period of about a week. Our voluminous notes and all the great textbooks, be it Gray's anatomy or Starling's physiology, etc. were familiar to us. Some books such as Boyd's pathology we practically memorized including the small print. Because I studied so hard and long in that first year I developed, what one might call, a nervous breakdown the following summer. This state made me so insecure that I almost did not return for the second year. That only a small number of pre-medical students qualified for entry into medicine, and one third of the medical class had failed by the end of the second year provided an impetus to study. Following these final exams, we retired to the nearest local beer parlor and sought complete relaxation.

Kirchner: The questions were not of the multiple choice type, or true and false, but rather you had to write a little essay on each question on the paper. Is that correct?

McNeil: Yes, that was the nature of our exams.

Kirchner: Did you have to participate in didactic examinations as well, and how were they carried out?

McNeil: Yes. For example, in pathology one would meet with Dr. Boyd, and he would be surrounded by specimens; some of these would be specimens from our labs, but others were new surgical or post-mortem material. I remember Dr. Boyd showing me a "bladder like" thing with a knob at one end. It was an enlarged prostate associated with a trabeculated bladder, the result of long continued urinary obstruction. I knew that my answer was wrong before I spoke, but my failure to think it out clearly was due in part to the stress I felt. I can still visualize his expression following my reply. Oral exams in anatomy were similar and those in histology and bacteriology were the identification of material as seen through a microscope or the appearance of the culture in a Petri dish. The clinical examinations were carried out at bedside, with the patient a curious part of the process. I think that sometimes we had studied too much. When a surgical examiner quizzed me on the causes of surgical shock I had so many classifications in my mind, and knowing as well this particular clinician's own classification, I could not seem to unjumble them in my mind and therefore speak rationally.

Kirchner: In the time that you were studying medicine Fleming's discovery was already known. Did you learn about it as a student?

McNeil: No, I didn't. Sulpha drugs were just becoming available to us then. I remember a professor telling us of a favorable response he had observed in a case of septicaemia having used the chemical mercurochrome intravenously. The first time that I can personally recall using penicillin was in 1944 when I was provided with one hundred thousand units for the complete treatment of gonorrhea in a bomber pilot.

SIX

Kirchner: Perhaps there is something more of interest that I might ask you at this time, and that is about the cost of education and how you might have financed it during those difficult times. As students, I believe you were expected to make a considerable effort in this regard.

McNeil: Yes. It didn't seem fair to ask your family to just continue paying at this stage for your education. We expected and we wanted to work. When I talked to my dad about entering medicine I told him I would expect to pay for my own tuition and if I could continue to live at home I would not ask for more. University did finish early in April and we would not return until about the first of October. That was a long time in which you could plan to work and earn. I believe there were other benefits from this break in that it was worthwhile to be separated from the institution — a kind of a sabbatical from which one gained physically and mentally. Both teachers and students were refreshed and ready to rededicate themselves. Students did a number of things but unless you were one of the few who had some other qualifications, manual labor, if one could find a job, was the most profitable. One of my classmates owned and operated a small grocery store through all of his college years. A few students, men and women, obtained work in the large railway hotels. These were the resort hotels like the Banff Springs, the Chateau Lake Louise, the Jasper Park Lodge, and even hotels in the East. The students who obtained such jobs worked as bellboys, bus drivers, or in the case of the girls, chambermaids and waitresses. It was profitable to drive a sightseeing bus at a resort, for I understand the wealthy guests could be quite generous. Brewster Transport's buses in Banff were driven by students and the drivers apparently had some great times, although I would wonder as to the amount of money saved. The resort hotel work was not available to most of us. It seems you were required to have some connections in eastern Canada to be so fortunate. During the depression years the opportunities for work were very limited, and the truth of my predictions to Dad as to earning my own tuition, as summers went by, was unfulfilled. Unemployment was rife and thousands of men in search of work were constantly travelling — "riding the rails". I used this mode of travel in a similar manner to reach Sioux Look Out, Ontario, in an unsuccessful search for work. I returned to Winnipeg

28

the same way arriving home dirty and hungry. The coal business did not operate in the summer, but I did busy myself there as I have told you. This situation didn't develop confidence in oneself, or help you develop your personality. Some of us felt we were a burden to our families. I know that I used library texts often rather than ask Dad or my brothers for the money to buy my own. In the summer of 1937, that is before I entered my 4th year of medicine, I did get a job. This was the last summer one could work, for after fourth year we immediately entered the hospital as a junior intern.

I obtained a job in Red Lake, Ontario, on a gold prospecting venture. To reach Red Lake I rode a freight train to Hudson in Ontario. Hudson was a place where freight to the gold fields in the north was transferred from the railway to large freight scows on the lake. The transportation companies operated fleets of boats which would tow several scows, loaded with the many types of materials, food, building material, machinery, etc., destined for mines and prospecting companies. The scows were "portaged" by means of a railway system from one lake to the next. The trip required crossing a whole number of lakes and portages before reaching the town of Red Lake. I approached one of these transportation companies at Hudson asking for the privilege to join one of their scow fleets in return for work I might do for them while we travelled. This opportunity was given to me and I proceeded on a fabulous journey. I wish that I could describe this experience adequately, for only one who has been in the north country could appreciate what I mean. Have either of you ever been in that north country? It is endless bush, trees and water and rock with beautiful starry nights. For about a week, I sat on those scows and I revelled in it all. I carried no food, but would have to move from scow to scow to reach the boat where you might scrounge something to eat from the galley.

Red Lake was rather wild and tough with a great deal of drinking and gambling and there were very few women. There was one group of women at Red Lake then and I recently read something of their story in a newspaper article. Some of the women in these houses became notable citizens later. This phenomenon is told in the story "Red Lights on the Prairies" as written by Mr. Gray. Their earlier profession did not prevent this and I personally observed this phenomenon in my practice later. I went along with the boys one night to the local bordello. This was an experience which I would not have wanted to miss. I had the opportunity to meet these people, to observe their personalities which ranged from the aggressive and vulgar to the quiet and humble. While visiting and at least buying the girls a drink, I could see the madam in the back room as she sat in deep subdued conversation with the notorious western Canadian criminal lawyer Walter Hagan. One girl (who said she was Jewish) I met again later at a V.D. clinic where

I was obliged to give her an injection of Mapharsen for her syphilis. I eventually did get a job and worked on the surface (not underground). The foreman was a "half breed" as we might call a Metis then. This man was formidable — tough, rough, and a heavy drinker, who expected a good day's work from every man on the crew, and most importantly he would not tolerate a "slacker". I weighed about 130 pounds and, as you might imagine, the heavy work of pick and shovel, lifting rocks, etc. was difficult for me. Gus, the foreman, I soon learned to respect. It became apparent to me that if I tried my best, he could find ways to make it easier for me. This reminded me of my math teacher back at Kelvin who I realized was saying the same thing "it was the effort I made, not the result which would earn his respect." Gus would see that I would get a break when I seemed to be too tired. This might be effected by telling me to "bugger off" and get water for the gang from some distant place in the woods. Gus would enjoy the luxury of having me, a medical student, massage his painful leg at night when he felt so inclined. I consider that Gus was one of the real "Class Acts" of my lifetime. When I came back to medical school that fall I was a different person; I was healthy and strong, had some financial security and a sense of dignity which had almost been lost during the depression. I had earned a tremendous amount of money, $4.00 a day plus my room and board, and I had spent almost nothing. It cost me $25.00 to come out of the bush by seaplane, as the only passenger, and was picked up on the lake in front of our bunkhouse. I now had this money to hand over to Dad and Maun that fall. I had won the respect of the whole crew, men of varying backgrounds, and the spinoff was increased self respect for myself.

Kirchner: In 1937, was the effect of the depression in Red Lake area still present?

McNeil: The depression was still very much apparent; many men were looking for work. Mining prospects offered some possible opportunity. The mines or prospecting sites were widely dispersed and on various lakes. For some it was necessary to travel by air, others could be reached by boat with a kicker (outboard motor). Red Lake was at least 20 miles long. One would see examples of empathy towards the unemployed. The manager of one of these camps, a "hard rock" geologist, couldn't offer me a job, but left me with a pleasant feeling when he kindly said, "Perhaps you can come back, something may turn up."

I learned other things too in that time. I do not know whether Gus ever had any schooling, but I learned from him some of the basic elements of geology. On the other hand our manager, a geologist, did not seem to know or care about what he was doing. He spent his time fishing. Under Gus's direction we followed the quartz intrusions through the granite. The gold was commonly found within the quartz.

The stringer was often apparent on the surface, but in other places the overburden had to be removed. It was necessary to drill, and then dynamite the drill holes, looking for the larger ore bodies. The mine owners to whom I owed my job did not earn our respect. They were from Toronto, and merely stock promoters. They arrived on a yacht accompanied by their girlfriends. I don't think the area has ever been fully explored. I still possess a good sized bag of high grade ore taken (not legally) from this prospect. I learned that a university education was not a prerequisite for knowledge! I have digressed too much I know. In regard to the depression the government camps were still in operation. These camps were situated in remote areas and housed hundreds of men whose remuneration was subsistence allowance. They were often employed doing work or development for projected provincial or federal parks. These conditions persisted up until the beginning of the war two years hence.

Kirchner: Could you tell me, as an educated young man, did you feel any resentment from these working men at the mines? Did they accept you as you were or was there a resentment towards the educated boy?

McNeil: Yes there was resentment.

There were three medical students in this camp, and we had obtained our jobs through some connection or friend in Toronto. The other men had been out of work and unable to earn their living for some years.

Kirchner: They accepted you?

McNeil: They accepted us to a point after a time, I think. By the end of the summer, I experienced some satisfaction in having won their respect. These men were, for the most part, European immigrants and chosen because they would be able to do heavy work.

Kirchner: It must have been a very interesting experience, even enriched our medical knowledge, having been in contact with this type of person and lived with them.

Kirchner: Did this interest in the subject of geology remain with you?

McNeil: Yes. It was fostered by the Calgary environment where, in the oil business, geology is so paramount. Meeting with patients and friends in the oil patch and having a little knowledge of the subject I think was worthwhile. "Hard Rock" geology where minerals are found was once thought to be quite a different subject to the study of fossil beds or "Soft Rock" where oil is found. As you well know, one is formed through violent phenomena and may be called igneous or fire rock, and the other, the residue found in ancient sea beds. The two types of geology are now considered related.

I took a course at the technical school in Calgary one winter in geology. There I wrote a little essay on "The nature of Granite" and

31

one of my classmates and I accompanied the Alberta Society of Petroleum Geologists on one of their annual field trips. Other non-medical courses I have enjoyed were in the Classics, painting and sketching, Egyptian hieroglyphics, and one in Astronomy.

SEVEN

Kirchner: Please comment on the 4th year of your medical schooling and then on the internship period.

McNeil: The third and fourth years consisted almost entirely of clinical medicine. I believe that our clinicians were very good, and that some were quite superior. As I think of our medical teachers then, they would have obtained a basic medical degree in Canada, but their graduate training was done outside of Canada. You expected a superior consultant to have had offshore postgraduate experience and to have appropriate degrees to indicate this. At that time it was not as common to train in the United States, but the great schools in the States were well known. It was at Johns Hopkins, of course, that our Sir William Osler was present for so long. It would be my understanding that for special training one might do some of the necessary study in Central Canada or the United States, but it would eventually require experience only obtained in England or Europe. We knew much about the great medical schools in England, in Ireland, and the Continent. The graduate training for pathology might be in Germany where Virchow was justly revered. Spain and Italy were known to us for the advances they had made in neuroanatomy. Few were conversant in French and so were denied the opportunity of training in their great centres. The training for obstetrics would likely be obtained at the famous Rotunda Hospital in Ireland, in Dublin. The influence of the London hospital schools pervaded medical teaching. The goal was to obtain the "F.R.C.P." London or Edinburgh for a physician, or for a surgeon the "F.R.C.S." London or Edinburgh. The Royal College in Canada only evolved in the late thirties. Our teachers regularly possessed the English degrees. Many physicians and surgeons had medical experience in the previous war and this was believed to be an advantage.

We attended lectures or clinics supervised by these men. I will mention some of them. Firstly, Dr. Lennox Bell (whose father had been a notable physician in Winnipeg) stands out among these teachers. He was a young and fine looking man who was able to stimulate a great interest in us for clinical medicine that is in contrast to surgery. To many of us internal medicine was looked upon with great respect. Dr. Bell (Buzz) was our teacher and also our friend. We often met with

33

him socially, often at his home. This was in contrast to those other, more aloof and less approachable, mentors. There was a good deal of drinking in medical school then, so much so that one received the impression that the consumption of alcohol was a prerequisite for one to be in the profession. Doctor Bell was widely acknowledged for his teaching ability. His whole career was devoted almost exclusively to this. The time spent with him was largely on the wards. He deservedly became the Professor of Medicine and then the Dean.

McNeil: As I was thinking about our medical teachers, I turned to a symposium prepared for the celebration of the 100th anniversary of the Manitoba Medical School. In this interesting story they speak of the "Winter years", referring to the pre-war and depression years of the school. This description is taken from the title of the book written by the Canadian writer James Gray. It dealt with the great depression in Western Canada. These were difficult times for Manitoba and for all educational institutions. The economic times were unfavorable but as I look back I do not think that we suffered as to the quality of our teachers. A later chapter in the same symposium is entitled the "Halcyon Years" and relates to the great support for education in the post war years. I would like to give you this little symposium for the Medical History Library, if you would accept it. In no way does it represent the complete history of the faculty, but it does provide a splendid synopsis of the development of the college. In recounting some of the names in clinical medicine I have mentioned Dr. Bell and would add Dr. J. D. Adamson, Head of Medicine at St. Boniface, Dr. H. Kitchen, Dr. J. McEachern, Dr. A. Hollenberg, Dr. C. R. Gilmour, the professor of Medicine, Dr. A. T. Mathers, the Dean, and also the professor of Psychiatry — an excellent teacher. In surgery, including the subspecialties I would think of Dr. J. Gunn, the professor of Surgery, Dr. P. H. T. Thorlakson, founder of the Winnipeg Clinic, Dr. C. E. Corrigan, Dr. Pit Perrin, Dr. A. W. S. Hay (a war time casualty), Drs. A. C. and W. F. Abbott, Dr. N. L. Elvin (Ophthalmology), Dr. A. P. McKinnon and Dr. M. A. Gibson (Orthopedics), Dr. M. S. Hollenberg, Dr. H. Greive, Dr. D. M. Bruser, Dr. O. S. Waugh. In gynecology and obstetrics, I would think of Dr. G. D. McQueen, Dr. D. S. McKay, Dr. Ross Mitchell, (The Dr. Ross Mitchell Medical Historical Library). I remember something about many teachers and I recall the welcoming address to our class given by Dr. Fred McInnes of the department of gynecology, and recall his words that we shortly would be introduced to a book, namely Gray's anatomy, in which, "If you cannot in the future find something that you did not know, you would always find something that you had forgotten." I recall, too, his first lecture in obstetrics when he impressed upon us the old truism "pregnancy is always a positive state and could not be — a touch of." I was speaking to Professor Audrey M. Kerr, the Medical Librarian at the University of Manitoba whom I understand is a good friend of yours, Mr. Kirchner. In talking about former professors, she said, "We can tell you the names of these people but I wish someone would tell us what they were really like." In this vein we, as students, spent a great deal of time in the library, and must always be grateful for that unfailing assistance. I have forgotten the names of the two lady librarians, but in private we would refer to the rather large lady as "Hypertrophy" and the very small lady as "Atrophy". In pediatrics I think of Dr. H. B. Chown and Dr. H. Medovy. The renowned Dr. Chown (notable for many research successes including the Rh factor work) is poignant in my memory, not for the research but for his warm, kind personality. To illustrate I will relate one anecdote. I had completed my final examinations in medicine when I was astounded to realize that I had misinterpreted the instructions pertaining to the paper on pediatrics. I was certain to fail — what to do? The principal examiner as listed on the paper was Dr. Chown. I boarded a streetcar and headed for north Winnipeg where the Children's Hospital was located. I knew the impropriety of such a step but my anxiety was great enough to overcome this fear. When I later found out that I had passed, (barely) my relief was associated with the pleasant memory of the warm, kind reception I had received on a hot Winnipeg afternoon, now a long time ago.

Kirchner: You have spoken of clinics and I understand that these were teaching exercises. What did you do in these clinics? I am thinking particularly of the surgical clinics on the hospital wards, and in the patient departments, but information on other clinical teaching methods would be of interest.

McNeil: The clinics were essentially learning exercises for the purpose of developing diagnostic skills. They were not demonstrations of surgical or medical techniques. As an example, I will try to describe a surgical clinic with Dr. Eddie Corrigan. Our group of about eight students would arrive at the appointed time at his office in the outpatient department of the St. Boniface Hospital. I can remember the feeling of tension I would have, as we would find a chair or gather around the room, looking for a place where we could see and hear well, avoiding, if possible, being too obvious and available for selection. Dr. Corrigan seemed to emanate an aura of "toughness" and in the teaching process he would use the student's error in judgement to bring about a more suitable clinical thought process. This experience was humiliating to us, being openly ridiculed with regard to a statement or conclusion. A patient would be brought in and one of us would be instructed to examine the patient. The examiner would not venture a diagnosis at first. The examiner student would be watched carefully as to the manner in which he went about the examination. Should you begin your exam palpating an area or a mass before carefully viewing the part might be your first mistake. I learned that step so well that much later on, attending a graduate course, I visualized the chest of the patient first before doing anything else, and was shocked when the clinician asked me to give him the diagnosis immediately. Had I been even more observant, I would have noticed that the apex beat of the heart was on the right side of the chest, and would have been able to say that the patient had a Dextrocardia. Dr. Corrigan would say little or nothing for some time. If it was a mass in the neck, the student would state the size, shape, consistency of the tumor, what relationship it had to other structures, whether it was attached deeply or to the skin and whether or not it was "fluctuant". When there was a general consensus as to the characteristics of the tumor, he or the group might venture a diagnosis. We might then be asked the characteristics to be found should it be a congenital cyst, an acute or chronic infective process, a chronic granuloma such as tuberculosis — actinomycosis, a primary or a secondary tumor, a lymphoma, or Hodgkin's disease. I think that you will agree with me that it was an exercise calling upon us to use all of our academic knowledge in this clinical setting. We often did not consider laboratory aids nor, in the one hour allotted, discuss treatment at all. I can think of another clinic where the surgeon clinician presented us with four or five patients who had been admitted for abdominal pain. One clinical tool we tended to rely upon was a book entitled *The Early Diagnosis of the Acute Abdomen*. One, of course, does not learn his surgery (other than the mechanical techniques) in the operating room such as the layman may believe. As a first assistant in the O.R. it might be worthwhile, but as a second or third assistant in an operation it was a waste of time. The lack of technical training in those early years was brought home to me one night when as a fourth year student, acting as relief for an intern, I was asked to insert a retention catheter in a female.

In an orthopedic clinic, the eminent Dr. Gibson emphasized his subject, the reduction of shoulder dislocation, by telling us of an incident. When the resident met him at the hospital and told him that he was unable to reduce the dislocation, Dr. Gibson said, "How fortunate you are; I have never seen such a phenomenon." I thought of that often later when an airman overseas was brought to me with a dislocated shoulder.

Gynecology clinics would be held on the wards and in the outpatient departments. With a suitable subject I have been one of the group of students to carry out a pelvic examination on the same patient. It was demanded of us that we treat a patient with all propriety and respect whenever we examined or questioned one. We had a great number of sessions regarding the management of abortion. This teaching was not the procurement of such, but management; the prevention of, and the proper treatment of the process when the process became inevitable.

We were not provided with any formal teaching in contraception as it was not an acceptable academic subject. To overcome this deficiency, we made private arrangements with Dr. McKay, the head of the department, to have an informal session with us on a Sunday morning. We did have a few sessions in Ophthalmology; a common trick in a clinical test was to ask that we discuss the nature of the disease, and the patient would have an artificial eye. I have a text (not in great condition), *May's Textbook of Ophthalmology*. It is dated 1900 and to me it is remarkable in that its description of the clinical signs and the differential diagnosis is almost adequate for today. Treatment, of course, is of interest. I would again be pleased to turn it over to the History Library.

Clinical medicine offered a great scope for the clinical approach. I can think of a session with Dr. Bell when we might spend a great deal of time learning to recognize the timing and the many other characteristics of heart murmurs. The rumbling diastolic murmur of mitral stenosis, the result of rheumatic fever, was more common then. We were keen enough to take the opportunity to spend extra time in the hospital, such as a Sunday morning, for more experience. The examination of the chest was most important and for this study we might meet with Dr. Adamson, a respirologist. While probably too many X-rays of the chest are done now, we probably did not do nearly enough of them. We were expected to recognize the clinical signs of consolidation, pleural fluid, cavitation of the lungs, and to know the significance of pleural "rubs", etc. We did expose ourselves to infections like tuberculosis unnecessarily. To use up time in demonstrating "whispering pectoriloquy" seems foolish now. For some reason I think now of Dr. Adamson asking us whether people with deformed chests suffered from more pulmonary disease. The words of the lesson remain in my memory, "Yes, because of the interference with bronchial drainage."

EIGHT

Kirchner: Could you now comment on your internship year.

McNeil: For the internship year, you were required to select a hospital and to make application to the internship committee of that hospital. A number of hospitals were approved by the university for such training. The places so approved were almost entirely in the city of Winnipeg or the city of St. Boniface next door. A few were permitted to apply for placings in Saskatchewan hospitals and I believe one person applied and was accepted at a hospital in Port Arthur, Ontario. The two hospitals in Winnipeg were the most desirable because of their proximity to the medical school, and of these two the Winnipeg General was the more desirable for a number of reasons. It was attached physically to the college and the staff were generally the most senior faculty teachers. One might, at the General, for example, have the opportunity to sit down to lunch with a faculty member such as Dr. Boyd or attend a lecture given by a notable visitor to Winnipeg. The university library was immediately available to the intern or resident at the General. The St. Boniface hospital was somewhat newer and the interns' quarters were nicer, situated a little distance from the hospital and close to the old Red River. There were equal amounts of patient "material" in the two hospitals. While St. Boniface had a number of good preceptors, there was, as I learned later, some serious weaknesses. To select a hospital in a city distant from a medical school would risk the situation where service, rather than education, would be the hospital's interest. Also, medical care should always be better where there is medical education in progress, I think you will agree. There was some concern, we thought, in the application process. Should you not receive acceptance at the hospital to which you first applied you might risk not having a hospital at all for the internship. While the hospitals were supposed to make it a secret type of a process, I was advised by Dr. Bell that should I apply I would be accepted at the General Hospital. For reasons that I would find difficult to rationalize now, but are probably related to my personal humility, I chose the St. Boniface Hospital. I had reason to regret this choice later. Dr. Thorlakson, the retired professor of surgery, and a friend of the family called me to his home that year. He wanted to know just how the General Hospital had failed to stimulate my interest. This was my first association with a Sisters' hospital and this in itself was a plus as I have spent my professional career almost completely in Grey Nuns hospitals. My first rotation at St. Boniface was at the infectious disease unit at a distance from the main building, where I was isolated for about a month. I had the opportunity to see diphtheria, smallpox, tularemia, anthrax, and all forms and stages of venereal disease. An entire ward was set aside for gonococcal arthritis; the pain and resulting deformities from this disease stand out in my mind. I assisted a surgeon doing a mastoid operation while there, and this must be a rare procedure nowadays. I approached that year with considerable enthusiasm and my diligence in the examination of the chest was rewarded by a tuberculous infection. My tuberculin test, while being negative when I entered the hospital, was strongly positive at the end of the year. No x-ray was done of my chest and no examination was offered to me. I suffered from repeated respiratory infections that year. I overcame the process, I suppose, by my own resources. Today a positive tuberculin test is of definite concern and the source of the infection would be carefully traced and active treatment offered, as you know. Then, it was our understanding, that by the time one reached adult life a positive test was the usual and desirable state. A positive test was considered to demonstrate immunity to the disease. Several of my classmates developed tuberculosis and required active reatment. To indicate the prevalence of this disease I have seen entire wards of tuberculous joint involvement. In speaking to a young active orthopedic surgeon recently I learned that he had never seen such a problem.

My lack of appreciation of that year was probably due to my naive expectations of the medical world. As an example, a surgeon who had removed probably thousands of appendices was unable to recognize the condition in himself.

Kirchner: Did he die?

McNeil: Almost. I remember his friend, a physician, relating to me the circumstances as to how the diagnosis was reached. In his French Canadian accent, "I lay my hand on de abdomen and den tell him, Louis, you have the appendicitis." I slowly developed some inner confidence as I lost respect for a number of teachers. The physician in charge of the intern services lacked any significant clinical ability but was served by a group of interns and residents as he pretentiously made his way around the wards. Successful observations of mine were treated by him with indifference, ignored, or attributed to some other more popular person. This tended to make me somewhat of a rebel or a maverick with an increasing dislike for some of the formal institutions such as might be called "the pecking order".

Kirchner: I think, Dr. McNeil, that you would be the first to acknowledge that your experiences at St. Boniface were not unique and that you would have seen similar circumstances often again.

McNeil: Indeed, Sir, and while such experiences evoke resentment which may last for a long time, they too are valuable lessons from which we benefit. The wound was reopened later when, as a result of an unfavorable reference, my application for fellowship at the Mayo Clinic was turned down.

Kirchner: I am curious to learn from your recollections as to the type and manifestation of disease prevalent then.

McNeil: Functional disease, such as psychoneurosis, did not seem as common then. I do remember, however, frank demonstrations of hysteria which in its most theatrical form would be rare today. The major psychotic diseases of course were present, but one had to be careful not to overlook a toxic process like lead poisoning or an infectious disease like syphilis. The large mental hospitals then were to a great extent occupied by patients suffering from neurosyphilis. I noted recently that the man who killed Lee Harvey Oswald, President Kennedy's assassin, suffered from this disease. Winnipeg had suffered through at least two devastating epidemics of viral encephalitis in the 20's and isolated cases continued to appear. There was a great deal of disability resulting from this illness. Antibiotics, including sulphas, were not available. The sulpha drugs did not come into our use until 1940. Management of infections and their complications consumed a great deal of our time. Bacterial pneumonia was a more ominous process and it was important for us to distinguish the anatomical involvement. Lobar involvement was almost always a pneumococcal infection, and bronchopneumonia almost always the result of a streptococcal invasion of the lung. The very effective antipneumococcal vaccines appeared (after tremendous research costs) only to become redundant with the advent of sulpha. Rheumatic fever was common as was glomerulonephritis, in relation to streptococcal infections. There were always a few patients on medical wards dying with subacute bacterial endocarditis. We could do little for these people; the fever, the pallor associated with anemia, the splinter hemorrhages in the nails and the characteristic heart murmur are still vivid to me. Patients in need of transfusions were obliged to obtain their own donors and these were commonly relatives. The donors would gather around the labs waiting for grouping and matching. Should a suitable donor not be found, a professional donor would be required and for this the intern was more than ready to act as such and receive the twenty five dollar windfall. The group "O" donor (which I am) was favored then, but this is not at all acceptable today as you know. While the enteric infections were controlled by public health practices under government supervision, cases of typhoid and others would appear. Laboratory measurements of electrolytes, acid base, and blood gases prevented the proper assessment and treatment of fluid loss. Intravenous fluids were prepared by the hospitals and the contamination of them with pyrogenic

40

bacteria made parenteral fluid therapy almost dangerous. Healthy babies developing diarrhea could died within hours from lack of, what would be called today, ordinary treatment. Heart disease at all ages, particularly the valvular types (like mitral stenosis) was commonly the result of rheumatic fever. The tremendous oedema associated with the resulting heart failure was treated with several drugs, the most common being of the mercurial variety. My physician son had never heard of a mercurial diuretic, drugs I have used so frequently. I cannot remember that coronary thrombosis was at all common then, although failure of recognition might have occurred. Concern about one's blood cholesterol did not exist. St. Boniface Hospital had the responsibility for treatment of venereal disease for the province of Manitoba.

Kirchner: Patients came from all walks of society?

McNeil: Yes, they did. It was not uncommon to find someone you were acquainted with sitting before you in a V.D. clinic.

Kirchner: These two, tuberculosis and V.D., were the main enemies of the time?

McNeil: Yes, and the acute infectious diseases. Whereas these diseases are uncommon now in the western world, when I went back in time with the hospital ship Hope (in North Africa) I saw all of these diseases again. At St. Boniface we served large clinics for the treatment of V.D. Those with acute gonorrhea received instillations of a silver preparation. As silver was used in the treatment of other diseases it was possible to see "argyria" where all of the skin came to be stained black. At these clinics, held two evenings a week, patients would receive intravenous arsenic or intramuscular bismuth for the treatment of syphilis. Skill with an intravenous needle was rewarded with long lineups at your table.

NINE

Kirchner: I would like you to comment further about St. Boniface Hospital; on the teachers, the Head of Surgery — was he a member of the medical school? What was his relationship with the school?

McNeil: I think it would be very much like it is today. The head of the department of medicine would have an appointment. Dr. Adamson was an associate professor. (I cannot remember at the moment who was Head of Surgery.) Other faculties would have lesser appointments. The university did not control the hospital, which some educators would believe is desirable now. Some of the senior preceptors were French speaking, the hospital being located in a French city. There was some lack of communication between the two large hospitals.

Kirchner: How was the selection of these outside faculty members carried out? On what basis might he/she be selected? Was it because he/she was heading the department of Medicine at St. Boniface and that he/she possessed sufficient qualifications? Or maybe because of some nepotic connection?

McNeil: There was some nepotism I am sure. The appointments at the Sisters' hospital would require the approval of the Sisters' governing body but I would think the appointment would be made only if the individual could demonstrate suitable qualifications. The hospital would be unwise to appoint people to senior positions who might not have adequate training.

Kirchner: And then that appointment at the university came by automatically.

McNeil: Almost, I would think. But that it was not entirely automatic was evident to me when I found that the man with whom I had so much difficulty relating to at St. Boniface did not have an appointment above that of a demonstrator. He acted, however, as a senior man in the department of Medicine.

Kirchner: You mentioned something very interesting. As a student you had to go along with the professor's ideas, otherwise you might run into serious problems. If a student had a dissenting opinion from the official standpoint then could that student be dismissed from the school, or was he only tolerated?

McNeil: No, I do not think that the school could be that despotic. I don't think that an official standpoint of the school existed. Amongst

42

the faculty themselves there were differences of opinion which could be quite intense. As I look back upon the faculty, with the exception of very few, I would regard our teachers with respect if not, indeed, admiration. We would regard someone such as Dr. Boyd with awe and consider him to be autocratic. I know that he would refuse to provide any sort of a reference for a former student, unless the student had first established that he could expect such. We were generally humble, possessing a respect for authority and experience, but don't think that we were fearful, that our future was held in some delicate balance. Through the power of the examination the school could exert influence. In the first two years of medicine, one third of the class was lost. Having passed the first two years, it was most unlikely that we could fail to graduate, unless from illness, or gross neglect of the work. I do not know whether I have answered your question at all well.

Kirchner: My question was referring in particular to some "dissenting" idea which was not the official one or what happened if a student criticized the teaching body.?

McNeil: I cannot remember that any student, around my time, took a stand which might be considered extreme or open to great controversy. We would not presume to openly counter the teaching of a senior professor.

Kirchner: It wasn't very good to speak up against the appendectomist?

McNeil: Oh no! This wealthy physician did not have our respect. He was listed, I notice, as a "lecturer" in clinical surgery. He was not taken seriously, nor did we consider that he had anything to offer educationally, but we would not openly condemn him. Should he have endangered life, someone would have taken action.

Kirchner: Would you comment on your impressions when you left medical school, how did you feel? Did you feel like a person of enormous power or more like a person who had very little experience and who knows very little?

McNeil: I would be glad to answer that, gentlemen. On the day I finished at St. Boniface, the hospital had no further need for me. My bed and room were occupied. It was a spring day and I went over to the medical school for some reason. The students had left and the place was deserted. There was no one to talk with, and I sat down on the steps of the old school thinking back over those five years. I recall my feelings at that moment. I have my M.D. degree, I thought, I am theoretically qualified to present myself to the public and they can place their trust in me. I do not possess such confidence. After all those years of such hard work and diligence, I should have had much more confidence in myself. Today, young physicians completing shorter courses with less exposure to the subject, less discipline, and less dedication than I exude confidence. No, I did not feel like one who

Don with his parents and brothers on Graduation Day, June 1939. Left to right: Hector, Ed, Annie, Don, Maun.

could wield great power. I cannot say as to whether this was a general reaction of other graduates. It was for this perceived need for more training, to bolster my confidence, that I had made application to Calgary for a senior internship. That confidence did not blossom in hospital and it was not until I commenced practice that I realized that I did indeed have ability. One must have the responsibility for judgement in his own hands before this can happen. I do not believe that this is obtained in the hospital setting.

I am not certain that this assurance the young graduate demonstrates today is justified. The graduates of the period of the late 1960's and early 70's, with their rebellious and arrogant attitudes, were sometimes difficult to relate to. I carry in my mind a cartoon demonstrating the forebearance of a young physician dealing with an older internist with obvious years of experience. This phenomenon is however as old as time.

Kirchner: There is one bit which I would like to know in respect to the teaching and learning of gross anatomy. You mentioned that you received a vertebra in a bag and by touching it you had to describe what it was and so on. In fact, as you now know, anatomical, gross anatomical learning is limited for the students. They are practicing on magnificently preserved cadavers, nicely prepared, and they do not have to touch a knife at all. What is your impression, looking back on your career? Was the long exposure to gross anatomy a useful experience?

McNeil: I think so. I marvelled at the human body and it was

44

wonderful to see the anatomy unfold with our dissection instruments. We almost revered our "stiff". I recall that it was the practice of a later anatomy teacher to ask the students to attend the final internment ceremony, when they had completed their studies on the specimen. We thought of it as our "entree" to this profession and believed that a comprehensive knowledge of anatomy was fundamental. Such complete knowledge of anatomy is probably not necessary. We spent more time learning neuroanatomy than many students now give to the whole subject. There are wonderful memories of the hours we spent in the dissecting rooms.

Kirchner: Was it very useful?

McNeil: I think so; I do think it is unfortunate that this change has come about. We could not imagine such an eventuality, and I believe that the present students lose a lot with their more superficial study.

Kirchner: Dr. McNeil, please tell us why, after finishing your university years in Manitoba, you decided to come to Calgary, why did you join the Holy Cross Hospital as an intern.

McNeil: After completing my medical course, and receiving my degree in Winnipeg, I had to make a decision as to whether I would enter practice or carry on further study. Some of my friends, in talking about graduate studies, were planning a journey to England or Europe for this purpose, and the threat of war did not seem to concern us. Some, however, felt ready and competent to start practice right away and some of them never did take formal training again. In my desire to have more experience, I could not consider depending on my family for financial support. We did, naturally, have some desire to earn some money. Hospitals were not in the habit of providing reimbursement to interns. A good hospital in Canada would not offer a salary to anyone but the most senior residents. This was one of the marks of a good hospital. The Calgary Associate Clinic was developing, and in their enthusiasm, had evidently prevailed upon the Sisters of the Holy Cross to offer financial enticement to interns. This offer amounted to the princely sum of $75.00 (1939-40) a month for the first six months, and if one stayed for the latter half of the year one would receive $150.00 a month. * This reward, I admit, influenced me and the other fellows to apply to this hospital.

* [Dr. Peter Jaron, a friend of Dr. McNeil and a fellow intern, remembers that $25.00 was held back from the $75.00 each month. The accumulated sum of $300.00 was paid out at the end of the internship year. Over and above their salary interns also received free board and lodging and free uniforms.] (Editor's note).

TEN

McNeil: I believe we were last talking of my early experience in Calgary and of the Holy Cross Hospital.

Kirchner: Yes, in fact, I would like to know specifically how did you join the Calgary Associate Clinic because your relationship with the Holy Cross was apparently deeper, at least at the beginning. So how did the two things come together?

McNeil: Four of us in the class came from Manitoba that spring to take up a rotating internship at the Holy Cross. My good friend and roommate from Winnipeg, Dr. Peter Jaron, was one and we merely changed rooms, not roommates. Peter has practiced surgery in B.C. very successfuly since. Dr. Cyril Walsh, following army service and a Mayo fellowship, became a surgeon at the Clinic. Dr. W. Ormand had a short life and career. We were provided with very suitable accommodations and they did everything possible to make us comfortable. The hospital had about 300 beds then. The Sisters' Hospital had grown up with the city and the story of sacrifice and devotion warrants recording in itself. Again, I would like to give the library a book which tries to tell the Holy Cross story. The hospital at that time was not well organized for interns; there were no staff patients such as I have described to you in Winnipeg. There was no ambulatory care, or a voluntary designation of patients for the purpose of teaching, as now exists at the Calgary hospital. All patients were private patients, having been admitted under a specific doctor and the care was therefore his responsibility. They tried to facilitate some degree of primary responsibility for us, but it did not work out very well. The Holy Cross has developed a program since, with which I was associated for many years, and this has had a successful history. I began to feel unhappy and I sensed that the year would be a disappointment as some things had been at St. Boniface, and so I resigned after six months. The fine Sister Superior of the hospital conveyed to me her definite disappointment. What was also a great surprise to me was that Dr. Macnab, (the senior member and the great driving force behind the Associate Clinic), not only expressed his disappointment but told me that it had been the intention of the Clinic to invite me to join them at the conclusion of my year at the hospital. This was indeed a compliment, but I had by this time agreed to take a position at Ninette

Sanatorium in Manitoba and they were apparently in urgent need of a medical man.

I was able to satisfy both parties by planning to spend several weeks at the Ninette Sanatorium with the promise that I would return to the Holy Cross and complete the year. Following several weeks at the Sanatorium I bought my first car (second hand with the earnings from Ninette) and proceeded to drive to Calgary in April of that year. That trip is impressed upon my mind and I would like to tell you something about it. The road was reported as impassable west of Regina by the Mounted Police. It was early spring and the frost had just begun. This would be just over twenty years since our family had moved from Estevan to Winnipeg, and the roads had not improved much over that time. Maunders had come as far as Regina because of his concern for me on this venture. The last part of the highway between Maple Creek, Saskatchewan and the Alberta border was very bad and one might well say impassable. I reached Maple Creek having driven through mud (on the Trans Canada Highway) for a hundred miles. I asked a man at the hotel if it would be possible to go any further and I recall vividly him spitting at the pot-bellied stove and saying, "Hell, I don't know, you've come this far, maybe you could if you were up early in the morning before the frost." I did just that and I recall how wonderful it was to see that sign on a grain elevator indicating Alberta Pool elevators.

Kirchner: Do you remember the names at the Holy Cross? Those persons who directed the hospital at that time? The doctors to whom you reported?

McNeil: There was no medical director of either hospital. The Holy Cross Hospital was administered by the Sisters' governing body and the Sisters' were guided by the medical executive which included all heads of departments plus some others. When, later, I was a member of the executive, I remember well that the now revered Bishop Carrol was always present, seated in the stuffed chair in the corner. The doctor to whom we would report to would likely be Dr. Macnab.

Kirchner: Macnab, yes, who was one of the founders of the Calgary Associate Clinic. But, for this period, I think that we might go step by step. So what we are looking at is that six month period which you spent in Calgary at the Holy Cross and the persons you mentioned that had a certain influence on you, from Dr. Macnab to Dr. Scarlett and others. Also, when you went back to Manitoba and spent a few weeks there. Please tell us something about that experience and about how you returned to Calgary.

McNeil: The tuberculous sanatoriums were modelled after the great European institutions where fresh air was considered to be so very important in the "cure" of the diseases. Indeed the axiom of the patients was "chasing the cure" and to do this they would be admitted to a sanatorium and remain there for months or years. Ninette was typical in that it was situated in a beautiful rural area of Manitoba, beside a lake, and the various buildings were dispersed over a number of acres. The patients' buildings possessed large balconies to which the beds could be moved. They would remain outside a large part of the 24 hours, not excluding days when the temperatures dropped to minus 40°F. They were served by a staff of doctors including an

Sanatarium Ninette.

internist, a surgeon, several general men, and regularly by other consultants. My work included general medicine, attending sessions where reviews of two or three patients' progress were considered, assisting in the operating room, and functioning at the large pneumothorax clinics held at least twice a week. The staff, including their families, lived on the grounds of the Sanatorium. Everyone followed the Sanatorium programs of resting a lot and eating most heartily, all of which were part of the recommended treatment for patients. The doctors and their families shared one table in the large dining room which was presided over by the superintendent. It was, to me, a valuable learning experience.

Kirchner: Tell us now of your work and experiences at the clinic.

McNeil: The following two years were the busiest and possibly the most illuminating portion of my career. The members of the group had a plan that they would employ a young doctor to live within the clinic building. Hospital emergency departments did not operate as

The Calgary Associate Clinic Buildings. Don worked in the two storey brick building behind the white house.

they do today. In our own offices, we had as much equipment as was readily available at the hospital emergency room. For minor surgery, or medical emergencies, etc., the patient might be instructed to meet you at the office, be it night or day. Our x-ray facilities, with the exception of a radiologist, were about as adequate as those of the hospital. I don't believe that a full-time nurse was assigned to the hospital emergency room then. As this live-in doctor, they provided me with a very nice room in the basement part of the building. The telephone operator, Mrs. Montgomery, and her husband, lived in an apartment next door to me so I could be reached by her, a patient, another doctor, or the hospital 24 hours a day. I rarely had an undisturbed night for the next two years. I was advised at the outset that my afternoon off was Thursday (like the maids) and that this liberty did not include the evening. One worked every weekend and holiday. The support I received from my colleagues and the response I received from my patients soon elevated my personal confidence level. The regard I developed for Dr. Macnab increased steadily. I learned to know him intimately and soon realized that his loud, seemingly rough, tough behaviour was motivated entirely by concern for his patients and the profession he loved. During that period I saw pathology, clinical material, and was a witness to a kaleidoscope of society. The dramatized popular doctors of the screen and television experienced nothing that I could not at least equal. In talking with me you asked as to whether

49

or not I made house or domiciliary visits. Yes, I did, and these interrupted my work in the office, my meals, my evenings and my rest at night. I would hasten to acknowledge the rich experiences such visits were. In addition to the support of my colleagues in and out of our office, I would like to recognize the cooperation and help I received from the Sisters of the Holy Cross and the nurses of both hospitals. The cooperation between nurse and doctor was superior then and worked in the interest of the patient. I came to know the police whom I might meet in homes, tenements, or even in the jail cells. I believe I was immune to being served a speeding ticket, and I enjoyed the free cup of coffee, and the companionship of a policeman in some restaurant in the middle of the night. The relationship and mutual respect between several disciplines was great!

While I do think that this sounds like exaggeration I must tell you that I became, in addition to my other work, the clinic's radiologist. Such a practice was not uncommon then; a physician might carry out radiological procedures without specific training in that field. My training consisted of a few lectures in medical school, and a few minutes of demonstration by Dr. Scarlett on the gastrointestinal fluoroscopy. My interpretations were dictated and became accepted as authoritative. I believe that my reports were amazingly accurate, as might be confirmed by operation, etc. The care which I gave to those exams risked radiation overexposure to the patient and myself. No one expressed concern regarding the amount of radiation I received. I wore gloves and an apron to avoid the skin lesions I had observed on other doctors who had done this type of work.

Maes: I would like to ask you about the charges made to the patients and how this was related to their ability to pay?

McNeil: I was advised by Dr. Macnab at the outset that no patient should be denied any service that we could provide for lack of funds. I never did concern myself about the economic aspects of the patient after that. I know the clinic business office made every effort to collect but their success rate was not high. Two dollars for an office call, three dollars for a day home visit, and five dollars for a night home visit was the rule. Other charges (surgical, obstetrical etc.) were a fraction of what they are today.

Kirchner: Was this the philosophy adopted by the Associate Clinic or was this just personal advice?

McNeil: No, this was the Clinic's philosophy. I would obtain consultation, admit patients to hospital and offer medical or surgical treatment as required without concern as to the individual's ability to pay. In hospital you showed regard for the patient's ability to pay by making the admission as short as possible. The hospitals would not deny a patient attention for economic reasons, but they too made every effort to collect their bills. Perhaps you would like to know my income?

I received my living quarters, office, etc. and $150.00 a month. I supplied my car with its expenses. This income more than doubled after a year. The latter salary exceeded my income as a Flight Lieutenant in the Air Force.

Kirchner: Would you tell us, Dr. McNeil, of your daily routine please?

McNeil: I began the day, regardless of what I had done during the night, at about 8 a.m. when I reached the hospital. Often we had a clinical meeting (rather like a clinical pathological conference) for clinic doctors. I would make an effort to see physicians, often in the operating room, for whom I might have seen a patient. I might seek formal consultation with some of these men or discuss a problem. I would then try to meet Dr. Scarlett and accompany him on his hospital visits or rounds.

Kirchner: This is which hospital?

McNeil: This is the Holy Cross. I've talked mostly of the Holy Cross but I would like at some time to speak of the Calgary General Hospital because I was a member of that staff and enjoyed my association with that institution. From 9 a.m. until 11 a.m. we made hospital rounds. I appreciated these when I could find the time. My interest was internal medicine from very early on. It would be necessary to visit my own hospital patients during this period as well. I might have admitted patients during the night and there would be a number of people under my care — perhaps ten at any given time. Following the rounds at the hospital, there might be a house call or two anywhere in the city (the community was much smaller then, with a population of about eighty thousand). I would reach the clinic roughly between 11 or 12 o'clock to begin the x-ray work. Perhaps three or four gastrointestinal series would be completed before I would read the x-ray films. There might be someone to see or a procedure to carry out in one of the surgeries, such as a paracentesis or thoracentesis. I would have my lunch sometime before 2 p.m. and be prepared to start my office after that. I was generally fully occupied in my office until late afternoon. Any part of this day might be interrupted by the need to rush out for an emergency house or hospital call. When an emergency occurred it was "get Mac to go", and I would drop what I was doing if at all possible and go. In the evening, on rare occasions, the Calgary Medical Society would hold its meetings. The hospital staff had almost no medical conferences. The requirements for accreditation for hospitals had not been established and so there was no impetus for that reason.

I attributed a great part of the success that I enjoyed to my knowledge of pathology as taught by Dr. William Boyd and the skills I learned in clinical medicine at Manitoba. Should you think I was excessively imposed upon by the Clinic, I suppose that would be so. In spite of fatigue and sometimes illness (resulting in hospitalization

On a country road, visiting a patient in the service of the Calgary Associate Clinic, ca 1941.

sometimes), I revelled in the work. I believe I did not weigh more than 140 lbs. at the time. I had almost no social life; for should I have been invited out, I would arrive embarrassingly late and would be regularly called away before the evening was ended.

Kirchner: It would be interesting if you would talk about these hospital rounds. You mentioned that sometimes you went along with Dr. Scarlett — how did this work? Did you have the opportunity to see the patients of other doctors or only your own and those of Dr. Scarlett?

McNeil: Dr. Scarlett picked up his notes on arrival from the hospital switchboard operator and among these he would receive a number of requests for consultations on "in-patients". He, too, would have patients of his own or patients of others receiving his continued observation.

Kirchner: For other doctors?

McNeil: Yes, for others, mostly Clinic doctors, but the patients might have been referred from distant places. A number of new patients were seen each morning. He didn't spend a great deal of time with them and I would often think it was not enough time. He did have a broad knowledge of "Medcine" as he abbreviated it, and one could learn much from him. A large amount of clinical material presented itself. He remained always current by attending many professional meetings, and also through keeping in touch with many of the notable authorities of the time. In addition to his dictated letters he would write several letters a day by hand, which he continued all of his life. The accuracy of Dr. Scarlett's diagnoses was pretty high and this is more remarkable in that the patients were not "worked up" by anyone else. The few interns in the hospital were spread far too thinly and the ancillary services, which are used so much now, were limited.

ELEVEN

Kirchner: I will ask you to carry on by telling us more of your early experiences of practicing medicine in Calgary.

McNeil: It was rare that I would be involved in surgical operating room procedures. I would carry out my own minor surgical procedures including the care of uncomplicated fractures in the hospital or in the office. I would at times be called upon for an anesthetic. The anesthetic gases were in use but I would probably use open ether (the liquid dropped on a mask held lightly over the mouth and nose) with the induction obtained in a similar manner by the more volatile and potent drugs such as vinyl ether or ethyl chloride. I did learn spinal anesthetic techniques, which became useful later when I was in the Service.

I did plan to carry out obstetrics but this did not amount to very much. Several men (the older general practitioners) did their own maternity work and the very capable obstetrician, Dr. Alec Fisher, did a tremendous volume of this work. My work usually involved individuals rather than families. The baby boomer phenomenon, by this I mean the families of the military service people, was only just commencing. Marriage, I believe, during the depression must have been curtailed. A mother who did come under my care was brought to the hospital with the onset of her labor pains, had an unfortunate result. When I was advised by telephone that the "cord" was presenting, my instructions were to have the mother immediately assume the Trendelenburg position. The infant dies unless the cord can be retracted. The nurse just didn't have the time to do this before my arrival some twenty minutes later. The obstruction to the circulation doomed the normal baby. The fact that her husband was, at the time, residing in a penitentiary did not alter her disappointment.

The acme of medical care then was the Mayo clinic. If the patient could afford it, they would possibly visit the Mayo Clinic in Rochester, Minnesota. It was not uncommon to hear that someone was "going through the clinic" and while this usually meant the Mayo Clinic it could mean the Associate Clinic. There was an effort to pattern the Associate Clinic after the American institution. At Mayo's, multiple consultations and examinations in several departments is the rule. The patient visiting the Clagary Associate Clinic might expect to see several

54

doctors too, and such practice was encouraged. We see this now, of course, in our teaching hospitals and while it increases public costs and captures the patient within the system for a longer period, it probably makes for better care. I was greatly surprised when I was first invited to see a patient in consultation along with several other physicians. When I observed that Dr. Scarlett and one or two other would also see the little girl, I thought that the inclusion of myself bordered on the ridiculous and I recall commenting as such to the nurse on the ward. Dr. Stanley, a former member of Parliament for Calgary, was the author of the little book you have now, Mr. Kirchner, *Fun in the Foothills*, and as you know, it records his early medical experiences in Alberta. I then saw his little patient one evening on the children's ward and carried out a careful exam on her. I was able to palpate a small tender tumor in the right lower abdomen and pressure on the tumor would elicit the pain in her foot of which she complained. Dr. Macnab entered the room just as I completed my examination and sensing that I had found something, was obviously challenged. He carried out a careful examination himself. The little girl made no effort to tell him anything more than he asked. He overlooked her "wince" when he pressed on her abdomen and so with no positive finding he capitulated and said to me, "All right Mac, tell me what you have found." Dr. Macnab complimented me that evening but I heard nothing more. She was operated on a day or two later. I apparently was generously praised to the child's family. I realized this had occurred when I began having frequent patient visits by people from the little girl's home town. Children can be the most satisfactory of all patients, with their uncomplicated personalities. I can think of another story but this rather a tragic one. Sometimes I carried responsibilities which were, I think, too much for a young physician. Dr. Scarlett saw this patient at home and did not admit him to hospital for some very good reasons. He asked me to carry on the further supervision of the illness, which was a frank lobar pneumonia. The patient was a doctor and at one time he had enjoyed a reputation as a capable surgeon. He was now an alcoholic and an abortionist, and he and his nurse concubine shared a fine home on the brow of the north hill. He obviously had quite adequate funds to provide for her and his own indulgences. He had been placed on the new drug Sulfapyridine and he improved rapidly. He was obviously so satisfied with my attention that he invited me to join him in his special work. He passed the "crisis" of the disease, a phenomenon not observed now, as antibiotics prevent this evolution of the disease. The recovery was interrupted by a severe complication, that of Delirium Tremens. It was indeed frightening to see this huge man fighting his attackers, the product of his hallucinations. It was necessary for me to use large doses of the evil smelling drug paraldehyde rectally, the common and effective treatment used. This new illness prevented me from continuing his Sulfapyridine, and it was necessary for me to keep him almost in an anesthetized state. He did not look very well at this point, and it was then that I was discharged as his doctor. His nurse advised me that the McEachern Clinic would now assume the responsibility for his care. While I was somewhat relieved by having this difficult problem lifted from my shoulders this situation did not continue. Dr. McEachern contacted me and insisted that I meet him at the patient's home. I had not had the experience working with our competition and I was not certain whether this might be acceptable to our office. I met Dr. McEachern at the home and I recall his solemn demeanor as he observed the patient, then his assurance to the nurse of his considered opinion that my attention to the doctor was indeed above reproach. The recovery from the psychosis was followed by a return of the fever. I immediately resumed the sulpha but the fever would not abate. It is possible, I thought afterwards, that I had overlooked the development of an empyema, the common complication of a pneumonia. When I was called on the telephone a few days later and told that the doctor was suffering from a very severe sore throat, I knew that I now was faced with this terrible complication, an Agranulocytic Angina, and that his bone marrow was seriously damaged, most likely an effect of my prescribed drug. I reached his home and now would not accept his refusal to enter hospital. At hospital it was found that he did not have one polymorph in a whole blood smear. I readily obtained every consultation I asked for including that of Dr. McEachern. Each consultant wrote a most careful report. The comprehensive reports dealing with the problem were supportive of me in every instance, but at no place was it stated that a disorder of blood cells existed. Perhaps this could be considered as a cover up, but the empathy demonstrated to me (having in mind the difficulties which I had to surmount) gave me the realization that I truly was a member of a noble profession. The patient died in spite of all my efforts.

Kirchner: You had no antibiotics at that time?

McNeil: None, other than the various derivatives of sulpha. I remember obtaining a medication called Pentanucleotide which allegedly contained several nucleic acids. One might expect it to be useful for a process of cellular damage, such as this one of Agranulocytic Angina.

Kirchner: I believe that you mentioned Dr. Merritt and that you have previously said that he was associated with Dr. McEachern. I take it that it pleased you to be associated with the other doctors whom you obviously held in high regard.

McNeil: Yes, I was glad to learn that I was not isolated from colleagues and whereas long standing differences separated some of my clinic associates from other physicians, these differences were not passed on to me. It might be of interest to you that I became the recipient of all of Dr. Stewart's (the abortionist) medical instruments and many of these were naturally of a gynecological nature. The blood pressure instrument was used for many years and I believe I still have it. This was the wish of his nurse and devoted companion. You realize that a physician would attend to his colleague for no charge. There are many stories I could tell and perhaps I could belabor you with one or two more.

I recall my very first home visit. In my insecurity, although I quickly found the likely cause of her illness in her lungs, the young lady found it remarkable that she was examined so elaborately, including a careful neurological examination. We had a most capable otolaryngologist in the office. Dr. Cabot was a Mayo trained specialist and in this work he demanded a careful logical clinical assessment of patients referred to him. He expected similarly a comprehensive survey of anyone you saw for him. On making a house call to one of his patients I was greeted at the door by some such exclamation as "Christ, what next!" I had a youthful appearance, I suppose. The patient suffered from the relatively rare disease Myasthenia Gravis. He had read everything he could find in order to learn as much as he could about this disease. He could not relate his present symptoms to this malady, but was certain that the novice before him would not be capable of doing so. He pretended, at least, that he was reluctant to have me in the house. I was just as determined that I would find the nature of the problem. When I advised him that he now suffered from Menier's disease and that this was not related to myasthenia, he was rather impressed. When this opinion was confirmed by Dr. Cabot he changed his mind about me and young doctors in general. I learned later that he was quite vocal in telling everyone who would listen that this Dr. McNeil was now the foremost diagnostician in town, exceeding in ability even the renowned Dr. Scarlett. You can imagine how this would compliment me then. I was called to a home where several families were living together. The families were related and the communal situation was probably motivated by the economics of depression times. The patients were two small children probably under six years of age. Each child demonstrated several raised red painful areas on their legs about the size of a quarter or larger. These had the appearance of Erythema Multiforme, and as you know, this is considered an immune response manifesting a recent exposure to a rheumatic process or similarly a recent exposure to tuberculosis. When I inquired about such possibilities and mentioned tuberculosis by name, the mother or mother-in-law raised her cane to strike me. I do not know whether she would have struck me or not as she was restrained by her daughters. A daughter-in-law who apparently was not that popular in the home had recently been admitted to the Baker Sanatorium having been found to be suffering from active tuberculosis. Tuberculosis had been described as a social disease and this story is such an example. My accuracy of diagnoses was not infallible and the following is an example. A man with abdominal pain was treated as a pyelonephritis, principally on the basis that I found his urine to be filled with pus cells. He went on to die from a fulminating appendicitis. We would often be required to do our own lab work on holidays, etc. We might do our own urinalyses and white blood counts should these be indicated. There may be white cells in the urine where, for example, the inflamed appendix overlies the ureter or the kidney, but an error such as mistaking fat globules in the urine for pus cells was a real possibility. During these two years, I was fortunate to deal with strange and weird phenomena such as the lady who presented herself with that incredible psychological phenomenon of pseudocyesis. Here the patient attempts to demonstrate to the doctor all the symptoms and signs of a pregnancy which do not exist. I treated a lady with thyroid medication for her myxoedema, but after assuming a normal metabolic state she relentlessly went on to develop hyperthyroidism although her medication had been cancelled. The stress and torment I went through was great, as you might imagine. I reviewed the medication possibilities with her repeatedly. At this point in time when as she was becoming increasingly ill and I was obliged to recommend thyroidectomy for her, she confessed. She had obtained tyroid tablets from somewhere and it was her perverted intention to cause me as much distress as possible. Another incident I can relate; a stranger to the city visited me by appointment, and this man was a model patient. He accepted without question my diagnosis and the treatment I recommended. He possessed a mass in one parotid gland which I diagnosed as the rather uncommon "Mixed Tumor" of a salivary gland. My recommendation for surgical removal was promptly accepted and carried out. Any direction from me was similary acted upon with courtesy and without question until my last one. I recommended follow-up radiation therapy and this was immediately refused. This advice had been a carefully considered one, a consensus reached after consultation with several doctors. When this advice was adamantly refused, notwithstanding repeated explanation of the importance of this step, I became angry. The story unfolded like this; he was a religious man and while travelling by train was accompanied by a religious authority of his church. This authority was alleged to not know anyone in Calgary, including doctors. He advised the patient to leave the train at this city and to visit me, whom he named. He further predicted the advice I would give and that the man must follow the advice up until the last step, namely the radiation treatment, which he then was to refuse. I do not support extreme examples of clairvoyance and this event did not alter my attitude. I am certain that any busy physician would have endless stories he could relate but these few have remained in my mind.

Kirchner: These experiences that you went through were during which years?

McNeil: This was the spring of 1941 through to the spring of 1942. I joined the Service then. I have said that my time was so occupied that I had very little opportunity for social activities. This was not quite true, as I managed to become engaged during that period. Mary Lou was a student nurse and often on night duty. When I might attempt to visit her on a ward such as the children's my courting would be hampered when she would hand me a noisy, unhappy baby to hold. She would regularly sit in the car (and perhaps snooze after a long hard day) accompanying me on my calls. It was necessary to return her to the nurses' residence before 10 o'clock as there was a curfew and being late would risk expulsion from the school. That is possibly an exaggeration, but the rules were strict in all hospitals in Canada, although possibly not as strict as in European or English hospitals. The girls worked a twelve hour shift and this might be longer if a supervisor found that something was not completely to her satisfaction. The ward shifts were not shortened or altered to make time for lectures. A nurse who had worked all night would find it difficult to remain awake during a morning class but she would sit in the warm classroom, properly groomed in her starched clothes. The admission standards for nursing schools were high. Academic and personal references of superior quality were obligatory. The girls were required to take the Florence Nightingale pledge, something of an anathema now and has I think been discarded by nursing educators. Despite hard work, tears, and despair, the voluntary drop-out rate was low. You may have seen a book entitled *A Lamp is Heavy*, written by a Calgary General Hospital nurse which tells about a nurse's life in a hospital training school. These young people soon learned to assume a remarkable degree of responsibility. There were no intensive care units and no surgical recovery rooms in existence. A student in her second year, assisted by one or two junior students, would assume the entire care and responsibility for an active surgical ward, containing sixty or more patients, on a twelve hour shift at night. A graduate nurse would float through the whole hospital and offer some resource service, but with patients in various stages of pre-operation or post-operation, her load was great. The nurses would be required to answer the needs of the actively ill patients, receive orders by telephone from doctors regarding new or problem situations, prepare a patient for the operating room and be prepared to receive an unconscious one from the operating room. There was usually one ward where the care of a polyglot of patients, represent the whole gamut of the derelict community, was collected and offered great challenge. The hospital training school and the heavy burden placed on nurses in training has fallen into disfavor, but many doctors and nurses do not support some of the nursing training programs now and the product produced from them. These young women, on entering the training school, may have been naive and immature, but after the trials of those three hard years they left the school as mature women, having both confidence and dignity. Graduates of Calgary hospital training schools carried on the profession all over the world (and at this time in military situations) with distinction. The rules might have been relaxed slightly for Mary Lou and me as the Sisters were well aware of my work and one or two of the Sisters might often keep her company while she waited for my unpredictable arrival. This romance flowered, of course, and following her graduation, and the completion of my period at the clinic, we were married.

TWELVE

Kirchner: How was the Clinic looked upon in the city?

McNeil: I think that is an excellent question. To many of the citizens of Calgary it was looked upon with great respect and some pride. Many people outside the city, particularly in Southern Alberta, regarded it as an institution which they would have the distinct opportunity and privilege to visit — voluntarily or by a reference from their doctor. It was possibly the most progressive institution in Alberta, second to that of the medical faculty at the University of Alberta at Edmonton. The Clinic then had roughly forty doctors and in addition to several doctors having general qualifications, specialties were covered by physicians having qualifications in Internal Medicine, General Surgery, Obstetrics and Gynecology, Ophthalmology, Otolaryngology, Urology and later Orthopedics, and for a while a Psychiatrist. After the war many other specialties were added as the Clinic grew. One general surgeon, Dr. Hugh Stuart, the urologist, Dr. Fred Pilcher, and an E.N.T. man, Dr. Cabot, were all Mayo trained specialists. One surgeon, Dr. Harry Morgan, was Edinburgh trained. Dr. Scarlett had done his graduate training at the Henry Ford Hospital in Detroit and at Johns Hopkins in Baltimore and other institutions. Dr. Harold Price, the pediatrician, received his graduate training at Johns Hopkins. Dr. Macnab received his whole training at the Bellevue Hospital in New York City. Dr. W. A. Lincoln, one of the early members and a founder of the group, held the esteemed degree F.R.C.S. (England). The building, with its central downtown location, was easily accessible to local transit and to bus and railway terminals. Some doctors in the city used the availability of the consulting services at the clinic for their patients and for themselves and families. A number of physicians, however, would have little or nothing to do with the institution. They ignored its presence, might speak ill of it, and indeed would not refer their patients. Some of the criticism stemmed from quarrels which occurred many years previously. As Dr. Macnab related these to me, I understood that the major quarrel began following a physician deputation which arrived at his office rather soon after his arrival in Calgary. They demanded to know whether he had accepted an offer to do a contract type of medical care for a commercial enterprise. He told them that he had not done this, but had been offered such an opportunity for his consideration. They seemingly would not listen to him, accusing him of unethical practice. Following this he perceived an alienation and a lack of cooperation from a number of the city doctors, and in particular those working at the General Hospital. The strong, aggressive personality of Dr. Macnab reacted to this state of affairs by a determination to support the Holy Cross Hospital entirely, to collect a number of physicians who were supportive, and form a group who would bring to the city capable young specialists who would assure the success of this venture. The Royal College at this time was in its formative stage and it was planned that it emulate the body in Britain. The College in its inception granted fellowships to Charter Members, and these consisted of notable people in cities across the Dominion. Dr. Scarlett, for example, was a charter member, as was Dr. McEachern, as were probably many others. Dr. Macnab was not so honored, and I believe that this disappointment may have motivated him to turn to the Mayo Clinic for his new associates and for continuing education for himself and others. There were other reasons that the Clinic did not enjoy a respected place in the minds of some doctors. It was said that should a patient be referred to this office that the referring doctor would not see his patient again. Clinic doctors, it was said, lacked the propriety of returning the patient to the original doctor. Some of these things were true, but there did exist a great tendency for a doctor to speak poorly of a colleague who was not closely associated. The Clinic would fall into this category to some other physicians. I know that Dr. Macnab regretted some of the factions which evolved, and would have liked to have restored his relationships, at least with the more senior and respected gentlemen. In defence of the Clinic there were men in practice who lacked basic skills and who did not deserve the respect of others. This we had learned, to our dismay, as interns at the Holy Cross. It might be remembered that there existed no audit committees and there were no mechanisms for peer review. Medical legal actions were almost unknown, and if there was some action, it was principally an action against surgeons. It might be of interest to you to learn that membership in The Canadian Medical Protective Association was maintained by means of a fifty dollar annual fee for all types of practitioners, and this charge remained at this level until very recent years.

As for patients, there were some who, of course, were satisfied with their own physicians, but there were others who stated that under no circumstances would they seek medical care at the Associate Clinic. They might have been influenced by some previous unsatisfactory experience at the Clinic, but I would think that more likely their distaste for the institution was passed on to them by some doctor, or possibly from personnel working with doctors. It might be remembered that

Clinic doctors had distanced and alienated themselves from the General Hospital.

Kirchner: Could you tell us a little more about the amount of graduate training that the doctors in the community possessed and how they obtained it. I realize that the residency programs were not developed to the degree that they are today.

McNeil: I realize that I am presuming to be an authority and some of my generalizations may not be valid universally. One could not obtain credentials in Canada other than fellowship in the Royal College. This latter degree was obtained, as now, by examination following an approved course of training. Examinations were held only in Eastern Canada. I cannot think of a Canadian earned degree (by examination) held by a Calgary doctor prior to the war. It was the common practice for a young doctor to associate with a practicing surgeon and to thereby gradually develop his skills and a reputation for competency. Some men, after establishing their practice, would leave their work in another's hands and seek a few weeks course at the hospital where they had originally interned. It was common for a doctor to take a course at a center like the Chicago Postgraduate Hospital. Here they would have the "hands on" opportunity to do abdominal surgery or cystoscopies as examples. This was also a common practice for a doctor working in a small town or community. He would leave a doctor (a locum) in his place during his absence. The course would have a substantial fee attached and the cost of travel and living added considerably to this. The annual meeting of the Canadian Medical Association was well attended, particularly if it was held in a western city. The academic portion of the C.M.A. meetings would be comprehensive and pertinent to practice of that time. (The C.M.A. Meetings cannot meet the broad needs of all doctors now.) We would be welcomed at meetings of the American Medical Association and their program would be very worthwhile. I am sure that many doctors carried on a lifetime practice in Calgary having never made any real effort to seek continuing education. This same situation may exist now, unfortunately, where a doctor carries on a practice lacking hospital privileges and therefore compulsory continuing education.

Kirchner: Perhaps now you would return to your story and tell us something about the personalities and customs of specific doctors, as you remember them.

McNeil: My recollections of people will be obtained from associations I had during my early years at Calgary and later when I returned after study. My recollection of Dr. McEachern is that of a rather diminutive, quiet man in his operating theater where there was barely a sound to be heard, other than the necessary requests for instruments. His junior associate and colleague, Dr. Bill Ingram, who possessed a very similar personality, would be helping him. Dr. Ingram could allow himself a gentle laugh, however, on some relaxed occasion. Mrs. McNeil often "scrubbed" for these surgeons and did appreciate them. "Scrubbed", of course, means acting as the primary nurse associated with the operation, and the nurse so designated played a very important part in the process. Nurses now have allowed trained technicians to take over this work! Dr. Willis Merrit, the senior internist in that group and a most capable one, was a large, heavy man, but his personality was similar: a solemn, reserved, taciturn man. The junior internist with the group had a personality at variance with his colleagues. He was quite capable and was apprciated even by myself in spite of this compulsion: he enjoyed providing a diametrically opposite opinion to his conversant or colleague. I considered him as the prototype of an iconoclast. He would enjoy negating recent respected opinion or research, such as the relation of cigarette smoking to heart disease. He produced difficulties for me later, when, after my graduate work, I would enthusiastically propose new modalities for the hospital. I recall him complaining to me that he was being obligated to purchase a farm to please his daughters to assuage their wish for having space to run their horses. This farm area now is much of South Calgary!

After what I have just said about the McEachern Clinic, the following would perhaps give a synoptic sketch of the members of the Calgary Associate Clinic. In the operating room the very large, anxious Dr. Macnab would have as his anesthetist either Dr. Stanley or Dr. Price and at any time he might bellow "George" or "Harold" or to the scrub nurse or operating room sister who would be standing by. The words used were very likely to contain explicit profanity. The anesthetist might be making demands and the whole room gave an aura of tension and clamor. Dr. Macnab would likely be assisted by Dr. Stuart who would mumble and it would be difficult to hear him at all. Following the whole procedure Dr. Macnab would visit every person who had been in the operating room and offer his sincere apologies. I believe his demeanor was tolerated and they knew it represented the anxiety and concern he felt for his patient. This Dr. Stuart, a tall, fine looking man, carried on his surgical practice in a manner such as he had learned at the Mayo Clinic. Following a later sojourn at the Mayo Clinic he returned to introduce thoracic surgery to Calgary. Dr. Price, of small stature, and a fighter pilot from the last war, was a more gentle, intellectual person, who usually acted as an anesthetist in the mornings and carried on a tremendous pediatric practice the rest of the day and night. He was one of three pediatricians in the city. Anesthetists were quite subservient to the surgeon, a situation which does not exist today. Dr. Alex Fisher, the obstetrician, carried on a large practice in this specialty and followed his patients with great devotion. He was a group "O" donor and would not hesitate to lie down and provide blood for a mother whom he thought had lost too much. Dr. Fred Pilcher, the urologist, spoke with a deep southern accent. I believe he was the first in Canada to carry out prostatectomies by the trans-urethral method. I remember his philanthropy — that of teaching groups of boys to fly their model airplanes. Dr. Harry Morgan, a close personal friend, carried on an excellent practice in general surgery. He contributed greatly to the affairs of the Canadian Medical Association and later became the President of the Calgary Associate Clinic. Dr. Aikenhead, a senior respected greneral practitioner, whose son followed him into the Clinic, was the brother of the professor of anesthesia at Manitoba.

Dr. Scovill Murray, another senior and very popular G.P., spent time avoiding other more aggressive doctors such as Dr. Macnab, so that he might indulge in his love for fishing. Dr. Murray was critical of me, when, after I and a consultant had done several rectal examinations, found a prostatic cancer in one of his patients.

Down the street, on the site where the Petro-Canada building is now, was a house surrounded with a wide veranda. This was the C.P.R. Clinic whose senior physician Dr. Stewart MacKid was associated with Dr. McLaren and several others. Dr. MacKid was of large stature as was his father who preceded him in this Calgary office. The C.P.R. maintained extensive medical services right across Canada. This group worked at the General Hospital entirely and were not well known to us. The railway was, of course, even a more vital part of the community then, than it is now. There were many other doctors whom I could mention such as Dr. Reginald Deane who was Calgary's first notable orthopedic surgeon; and Dr. Fred Campbell (who showed me my first "rose spots" of typhoid fever), but I believe that I shall stop here.

Kirchner: Will you tell us please where these clinics were located? The McEachern and the Macnab Clinics? You have told us of the site of the MacKid offices.

McNeil: The Calgary Associate Clinic was on Sixth Avenue where Bow Valley Square is now located. It was a two storey building, but its various sections were built at different times, so it was a rather complicated structure. The pharmacy, the business offices, the reception desk, Dr. Macnab's office, surgery, Dr. Pilcher's office, x-ray, and my office were all on the main floor, and that level was a busy and rather noisy place. The McEachern Clinic was situated latterly in the Medical Arts building at Sixth Avenue and Third Street West downtown. The Medical Arts building wasn't built until after the war, so the McEachern Clinic and many of the professional people were situated in the Greyhound building prior to this, and the one which preceded it, which was the Southam building.

Kirchner: The actual Greyhound building?

McNeil: Yes, in the actual Greyhound building. The lowest floor

65

was the bus station. There were, of course, no shopping centers and with the exception of Drs. Bouck and Brodie who had offices on First Street West about Thirteenth Avenue, all doctors maintained their offices downtown. The professional and hospital office buildings appeared much later.

Kirchner: So even in that time there was an established affiliation with hospitals? The Associate Clinic largely used the facilities of the Holy Cross, the MacKid Clinic that of the Calgary General, and what about the McEachern Clinic?

McNeil: The McEachern Clinic used the facilities of the Holy Cross almost entirely. The Associate Clinic would occasionally admit patients to the General, but they were not very popular there and were unable to exert their influence to the same degree as they would be able to at the Holy Cross. The estrangement was essentially between the medical staffs. I joined the staff of the General Hospital in 1940 so at this moment I think I'm almost the oldest member of the Calgary General Hospital staff. I was made an honorary life member at the General a year or two ago. I did a certain amount of my work at the General from the onset and I have always appreciated my association there. Earlier, some of their facilities were obsolete, and this would influence one's choice of hospital. Some of the senior nurses at the General, who might at first seem tyrannical, earned the respect of all. I might just mention Miss McDonald as one such person. Should I require any service, including a bed, (when the hospital was stated to be fully occupied) the wish would truly be her command. I was very happy indeed to attend the reception a few years ago held in her honor. The Clinic employed many nurses, graduates of the General Hospital, which attests to the quality of their training school.

The isolation hospital for Calgary was the old second edifice built as the Calgary General Hospital and it still exists on Twelfth Avenue East. A number of us spent long difficult hours there during some of the later polio epidemics which visited Calgary. Mr. Jack Peach, who writes about early Calgary, has a great deal of information on the development of the hospitals.

In a recent letter Sister Cecille Leclerc (the esteemed director of the school of nursing at the Holy Cross during the fifties and sixties) reviewed a little of the history of the Gray Nuns and particularly their contributions to Calgary. She tells me that archives do exist in Montreal pertaining to all of the sisters' hospitals including the Holy Cross. To mention the names of a few of the sisters I knew: Sisters Letourneau, Leona Breux, Ste. Crois, Garneau, Noulet, Meyers. This is small acknowledgement of some wonderful colleagues and friends.

Kirchner: It would be very interesting to learn something about your affiliation with the Calgary Associate Clinic. Under what sort of contract did you work there?

McNeil: Your questions, Sir, are indeed poignant. The contract stipulated that I would work at the Clinic on a trial basis for one year. That was in 1940 and the opportunities to find employment as a physician were not much better than for any of the occupations at the time. The old depression still lingered. One expected to join the Service at some point but there was no feeling of urgency about it. To open one's own office was a very costly consideration. I do not believe a bank would be sympathetic to your needs, as they were not for many years after the war, and medical qualifications did not seem to have any security value. One learned that doctors' offices were often the site of a card game, as the demand made on the time of many physicians was not that great during the thirties. The early requirements of the army were easily met by doctors who had experienced too many years of hardship.

Kirchner: So you were salaried then?

McNeil: Yes. I think I have mentioned this small salary before and that seems distinctly less when you realize that I supplied my car. It was of considerable satisfaction to me when this amount was doubled after a year. This increment followed my humble question to Dr. Mcnab as to whether or not it was the intention of the office to hire me again after the completion of my year. I recall being so impressed by the promptness of the membership's response and the concern they displayed as to my possible departure. I took it that there must have been an immediate meeting of the membership to discuss my future with the office.

Kirchner: Did this situation persist or did you at a later time become a full fledged partner in the Clinic?

THIRTEEN

McNeil: I resigned from the Clinic after two years having two intentions: one to marry, and the other to enter the R.C.A.F. I was favored with a Clinic dinner and a presentation. Among the number of kind things which were said to me, I was assured that I would have a place at the Associate Clinic when I returned and for the rest of my life. At this and another party they acknowledged Mary Lou. It might be of interest to tell you that the reception following our wedding was held at Dr. and Mrs. Harry Morgan's home.

Kirchner: In which year?

McNeil: This was in '42.

Kirchner: At the end of 1942?

McNeil: No, in the spring of '42. Calgary was a very busy military community in wartime and the numbers of servicemen grew steadily following the outbreak of war. In the autumn of 1939 the first enlisted men I saw stand out in my mind — they apparently did not have enough regulation uniforms and so the men were issued with various "make do" items. One of these was a hat like a pith helmet such as one remembers the soldiers in India and the tropical colonies wearing. The hats were not the substantial ones you might remember, but were made of a paper like product which tended to disintegrate with the weather. Fortunately, the winter in Calgary (my first) was beautiful and warm. I believe that same beautiful weather was enjoyed over most of Europe for many months in that year. The building of military installations soon became evident. All of Canada became the site of the Commonwealth Air Training Plan. The present international airport (McCall Field) was a British R.A.F. base entirely. The No. 3 R.C.A.F. service flying station was situated just south of Currie Barracks and the control tower and many hangars remain today. A large air force equipment centre was placed at Ogden. Elementary flying stations developed around the city and more service flying schools were found north and south of the city. Prisoner of war camps were present in the regions of Banff and Canmore. I have talked to you before, Mr. Kirchner, about the book written by a Calgarian, *Behind Canadian Barbed Wire*, and it tells of P.O.W. camps in the mountains in the first world war. It was rather hard on soldiers captured in the desert to be "under canvas" in winter time at such places. I did have the opportunity to see one of these camps and the prisoners at first hand.

Many of the air crew in training were from other countries. Australians and New Zealanders were particularly popular with everyone, especially with the girls. These aircrew, including the English, the Free French, etc. were hand-picked men who would have been required to meet high admission standards before they left their own country. They were indeed good looking, charming, mischievous fellows. I can remember learning of one or two of the prominent girls in the city who developed the usual problems.

Kirchner: You have given a little description of Calgary in wartime. We would like to hear something about your story in the air force.

McNeil: I was first assigned to the recruiting centre at Calgary, where one was impressed by the strong motivation of recruits to obtain actual flying training (in any capacity), and the great disappointment should they fail for some reason, like on medical grounds. I was posted from there to an initial training school in Toronto of the type required for all flying personnel. Here we learned the basic physics of flight and the reaction of an airfoil to every possible force. We had some introduction to meteorology, aircraft recognition, runway patterns, etc. This was the first time that I thought much about occupational disease. We were made aware of the dangers to personnel inherent in the industrial processes of aircraft maintenance. We had the opportunity to experience the effects of altitude upon the accuracy of intellectual processes by being enclosed in a decompression chamber simulating various altitudes. We saw the mechanics used and the methods of applying various "G" forces to the human body. We considered the important characteristics of clothing which might oppose "G" forces, or those clothes electrically wired for warmth. The planes were not heated and the big bombers were drafty and cold. The use of, and the requirements for, oxygen for aircrew was reviewed. The dangers of fatigue and the psychological effects of confidence in other crew members and equipment were all considered. Some basic military training was provided such as the use of a revolver, etc.

At I.T.S. we had opportunities to meet doctors from across the country. In the west, physicians then were largely graduates of western universities and only rarely were they from eastern institutions. This experience was interesting and sometimes a revelation. Doctors from Maritime Canada and the smaller colleges were very easy to relate to and our personalities seemed to mesh very easily. The University of Toronto (the largest enrollment in the British Empire) graduates, because of their tremendous numbers, were often overwhelming. They seemed more insular in their thinking and often lacked knowledge of the rest of Canada. A young medical officer who, on receiving a posting to a Winnipeg station, expressed serious concern as to the type of clothes

69

he would need in that frigid climate. While having been raised in Winnipeg, I have hardly been more aware of the "cold" than I was that spring in Toronto. I attributed the viral pneumonia I developed to the Toronto weather. My first winter in Britain was probably worse in this regard. Western people, who in a large part had emigrated from Ontario over two or three past generations, were more familiar with Eastern Canada. We had learned of Ontario from our families and from our history books whose content dealt to a large degree with this part of the country. We taunted U. of T. graduates about the special course we said they received! From this training school I was sent to Fort McLeod in Southern Alberta. Fort McLeod is interesting, for it was, at one time, planned that it should be the capital of Alberta. It was the northern end of the infamous "Whoop Up Trail" through which whiskey was moved by the traders from Montana. Here, of course, was situated the first R.C.M.P. fort. This flat prairie area was very suitable for a Service Flying Station. The winds were so strong from the west that planes would be almost motionless as they came in to land, although their flying speed as indicated by instruments would be the normal sixty or seventy miles an hour. This large flying school was one of several in the vicinity, there being one at Claresholm, Pierce, Medicine Hat, Vulcan, and at an elementary school in Lethbridge. We enjoyed the association with flying personnel and still maintain happy relationships with a number of the families. The doctors would be called to runways frequently to attend accidents, or because of alarms raised in regard to anticipated problems. I could usually obtain a flight to some distant place such as Moose Jaw, Calgary, etc. without too much of a problem. This flying was encouraged and we would receive extra pay (two dollars) for each day we flew. The mess committee has been known to land a plane in Kalispell, Montana when the rationed spirits were running low. An unhappy civilian barman decided to inform the R.C.M.P. of the presence of this American liquor in our bar. When the officers were tipped off by a policeman (an honorary member of the mess) it was necessary to keep an aircraft in the air for the next twenty-four hours except for refueling stops.

Our station hospital was large with probably seventy beds, and we received patients from the surrounding stations. Emergency and elective surgery was carried out by two capable surgeons: one, Dr. David Bruser, who was decorated for his work in Canada and who later has enjoyed an outstanding career as an orthopedic surgeon in Winnipeg, and the other, Dr. Rus McManus, a good friend and later a colleague in Calgary. During my two years at Ft. McLeod I did general work and in the operating room I was usually the anesthetist. My spinal anesthetics were variably successful, with the result being worrisome when the neck might be included in the area of anesthesia or when only the toes were anesthetized. The duties of a medical officer included venereal disease prevention and education. The work was heavy at times when one was required to spend long hours in the O.R. or attend the site of a crash often at some distant place. Of course one learned a great deal. Just one incident comes to mind — a man whom I had seen and whose throat didn't improve with the treatment, so I sent him for consultation. The older E.N.T. man in Lethbridge advised me in his report that this throat abnormality represents the "mucous patches" of the secondary stage of syphilis. This reaction occurs about three months after the initial infection and was easily diagnosed by this older doctor; but it was a good lesson to a younger man.

Kirchner: What were your living conditions: did you live right on the base?

McNeil: No. I stayed on the base only when on call. Mary Lou and I had, at first, a house without running water. The open door of the outhouse situated, as it was, at the end of one of the runways provided an excellent pastime. At a later time we revelled in the luxury of a one room motel. You might realize that it was great as a young married couple to have time together in wartime. The need for support people (not airmen) including medical officers in Canada was so great that the chances of overseas postings were small.

I was thrilled one day to receive my orders for overseas posting. The communication was brief providing no indication of where I would be going, but instructing me to report to the air force staging unit at Lachine, Quebec. After only a day or two at Lachine, we boarded a troop train for Halifax. We moved directly from the train onto the boat. This beautiful liner, the "Mauritania", converted as a troop transport still retained evidence of its peacetime opulence. The ship was heavily loaded with troops. It was not to be a pleasure cruise and I was directed to assume the medical responsibilities of the sick bay or ship hospital on "D" deck. I never did learn just what the duties of the ship's medical staff were, as I never saw them again on the trip. There was a lot of sickness, and infections spread rapidly with people in such close quarters. Sea sickness was a major problem and men had to be repatriated because of continuing disability resulting.

Kirchner: Did you have rough time sailing?

McNeil: As an officer I can't say that I did, as compared to the other ranks. The officers were provided with a stateroom which held about ten men, the same as a couple might have in peacetime. We were served our meals in the dining room whereas the troops received their food out of large buckets and ladled onto tin plates. On the lower decks with artificial light and minimal ventilation, it was understandable why men would develop seasickness. I believe most would say, however, that it was a wonderful experience. We weren't allowed on deck at night. No light could show in any manner. We were advised daily at lifeboat drill of the dangers present from U boats and warned about our behavior. On the fore and after decks American servicemen manned anti-aircraft and other types of guns ready to offer some protection for the ship.

FOURTEEN

We arrived at the harbor in Liverpool. I will try to describe my observations and my reactions for the first few days. What an experience to arrive in a country in wartime! Many have shared this situation including, perhaps, yourselves, gentlemen. As I gazed from the ship that morning, I saw this great harbor and observed that we were surrounded by ships of all types. The freighters had obviously arrived a short time before us as they were still loaded, and their decks were crowded with airplanes and guns. These planes were military types and there had been no effort to cover or camouflage them. Two great battleships lay just next to us. They were very low in the water compared to our troopship which towered several stories above them. I had in mind that they were the King George the Fifth and the Prince of Wales, but I think this is wrong as I do believe that those two battleships had been sunk earlier in the China Sea. I was impressed with the banter which took place between servicemen on our ship and these seemingly happy "tars" on the naval vessels. The shore and the docks around us, with their warehouses, were shabby, dirty, heavily damaged, and some buildings were obviously missing entirely. We did not leave the ship until one or two a.m. the next morning and then were moved to a large warehouse. We were picked up there by a transport driven by a pretty blonde girl, a WAC (Women's Auxiliary Corp). This girl stands out in my mind because of her Lancashire accent and by her friendly, happy talk as she made her effort to welcome us. This same kind of "fun" type of reception was repeated often as we continued on our way.

We left Liverpool in the dark by train and the next delightful experience was to wake up and see the beautiful English countryside from the train window. I have been to Britain several times since, but this first visit is imprinted on my memory. We arrived next at a staging area at Gloucester, a very historical city with its great cathedral. I was introduced here to England's damp and cold, to brussel sprouts and English pudding, and to being asked as to when I wanted to be "knocked up" (wakened). The cold was emphasized when I looked for the night table in which I had placed things the evening before and it was no longer there. I found my things intact, and then I found a few pieces of my wooden table beside one of the stoves in the barrack! We moved on to London next, and I experienced my first blackout and air raid that evening. The air raid occurred as I journeyed across the city in this blackness to visit Mary Lou's relatives. The home I visited had not had a direct hit, but only the kitchen and perhaps one other room were lived in. The rest of the house was all somewhat lopsided and the doors and windows did not fit. The uncle told me of the son he had lost over Germany with the R.A.F. He took some pride in, and demonstrated the superiority of, his air raid shelter over that of his neighbors. As I tried to find my way around the city that night I was impressed by the helpfulness and friendliness of everyone I met. I had a similar feeling one night in New York many years later — where in a total power failure the city was in blackness. The people there demonstrated the same warmth and helpfulness that I learned to expect in London and other cities of England. I had occasion to be in London many times again and found it to be the "London Town" as this fascinating city is often called. Mr. Churchill referred to the city by that term when he welcomed the sailors back after the sinking of the Admiral Graf Spee at Montevideo. The V1 and the much worse V2 rockets were still great perils at the time. I believe that most everyone who anticipates entering an area of personal danger, while not necessarily fearing that he could lose his life, would have anxiety as to how he might react under such circumstances. The example demonstrated by the ordinary people and the servicemen I met rather quickly removed any trepidation I had. The anti-aircraft batteries set up in the streets of London were ominous, but seeing the thousands of people with sleeping arrangements in the London tube stations and observing their indifference and good humour about it all was fascinating. London streets were as they always are, crowded and active. The population was swollen by thousands of men and women in uniform. The London theater was perhaps as busy then as it is now. I attended several plays over the next two years and think of "Blithe Spirit" and "Arsenic and Old Lace" as just a couple of these. One theater, The Windmill, a burlesque show, had a tremendous record of never missing a performance over several years in spite of the Blitz. During the day service people did all the touristy things — the Tower of London, Buckingham Palace, Westminster Abbey, etc. as is done today.

Kirchner: You were in uniform?

McNeil: Yes. I was a Flight Lieutenant (comparable to the rank of a Captain in the army). The object of going to London was to receive direction or posting to some air force unit. One might be sent to a tactical unit or a bomber unit. A tactical posting would take you to a fighter station, likely in Europe, but a bomber station would be situated in England; however, either one could be in any war zone, including the Mediterranean and the Far East. At the Canadian Air Force headquarters, situated in Lincoln's Inn Field (known for its law

74

chambers, etc.), I was issued a temporary British medical license (which I have kept) along with other necessary documentation.

I was posted to the headquarters of Number 6 group, an R.A.F. unit composed largely of Canadians, situated, I think, the farthest north of all bomber groups. The various stations or aerodromes making up the group were dispersed throughout Yorkshire around central headquarters. This central unit was a castle called Allerton Hall. The castle and its surroundings (an area of about a quarter section in size), was enclosed by a high stone wall. The estate, called Allerton Park, was situated near the lovely town of Knaresborough, not too far from the historical and walled city of York. The castle was probably quite modern, as castles go, and had been the residence of Lord Stourton and his lady who were presently housed in a more modern building, the priests' home nearby. Allerton Park (the area enclosed by the wall) contained beautiful grounds which included a lake with little rivers and bridges. Mary Lou and I have since visited Allerton Park and I tried to show her the things I have talked about. I know that there were lots of fish in the lake as fellows soon learned to poach. I have a picture of a huge pike being held in the dental chair with its mouth open as if it was to receive dental care. The castle itself contained the nerve centre for the entire bomber group of perhaps a thousand aircraft. The main control room was off limits to most personnel but here the operation of all aircraft was monitored constantly. The living quarters for all the staff on the station was peripheral to the castle, but within the walls, including my area, the station hospital. These buildings, as they were on most stations, were "Nissan" huts made from corrugated iron and the half circle of the roof and walls was placed on cement slabs. My hospital was shaped like an H with wards on one side and services on the other. On the ward side there were private rooms used for isolation, etc. and two multiple bed wards, one for females and one for males. The offices, treatment rooms, pharmacy, and dental offices were situated on the other side. Other than myself, there was a nursing sister and a staff of about ten other ranks, some of whom would have "sick room attendant" qualifications. My quarters were in the hospital and I must say they were very comfortable. I remember the nursing sister telling me one morning that the airmen in the big ward had said they could sleep better if the damned M.O. in the next room would not keep rattling his stove all night! As a medical unit we were supplied with all the coal we wanted, a situation which did not exist in other buildings or barracks. There were no fires, for example, in the officer's mess until supper time.

Although this sounds very comfortable, living as we did and surrounded by some of the most beautiful countryside in the world, (now sometimes referred to as James Herriot country) we were aware that this was a war zone. At any time looking upward you could see any type of aircraft exhibited in the wartime books today. About two o'clock in the afternoon, the planes of our group would appear in the sky and these hundreds of planes would circle for 3 to 4 hours in order to gain the altitude they required before they headed east for Germany. We might learn later, confidentially, of the number which did not return. Errors are always possible. During one German air raid on our station there was total blackout with the exception of the main operational control room at the castle where the drapes had remained open throughout the event. It is recorded that 55,000 R.A.F., which included large numbers of Canadians, lost their lives from bomber command. These great planes (Lancasters, Halifaxes, and Stirlings) with a crew of eight were being lost in numbers like ten or more each night from our group alone, even at a time very near to the end of the war in Europe.

I, as the medical officer at this station, was responsible for the medical care of its staff, the hygiene of the unit, and the administration of the hospital and I was, in turn, to report to the commanding officer. My patients were, in a large part, senior officers and airmen who had carried out one or more tours (thirty missions over Germany) as pilots, navigators, observers, and bomb aimers. The Air Vice Marshall McEwen (Black Mike as he was called) was housed next door to the hospital. It was interesting to work with these splendid men and others such as army liaison, civilian and military intelligence personnel, aircraft supply, and other equipment authorities attached to the group. There were large numbers of technical and office workers here at Allerton Park and many of these were W.D.'s (women's division). The Senior Medical Officer for the group, a Wing Commander, was present at the station and this very satisfactory circumstance permitted me to have relief for medical courses, or leave, and I took advantage of such opportunities.

Kirchner: Would you comment about the spirit of the crews?

McNeil: It was very good. I often visited one of the big aerodromes, where in the early morning the crew would be collected around their aircraft waiting for possible takeoff in the afternoon or later. These young men were full of enthusiasm, ready and happy to crack a joke, or kid you as you passed by. When one reads one of the books such as *Thousand Will FAll* and learns of the intensity which these boys applied to their long aircrew training, you realize that, to be at this stage in their military life was the culmination of long, demanding preparation. You also knew that they considered themselves the fortunate ones. The crew would busy themselves at various jobs or they might be painting a new sign on the nose of the aircraft, bringing up to date the number of bombing trips the plane had made. There were other decorations on the aircraft such as a pin-up girl, a sardonic one portraying what they might accomplish in their war, a cartoon character such as Bugs Bunny or an indication of where in Canada the crew originated. Later in the morning the planes would be lined up on a peripheral runway, motors running, waiting for their turn to take off. The lines of planes would exceed the busiest civilian airports of today. To lose one's life was to "go for a burton" or "to get the chop". Such terms became widely used and "getting the chop" became slang for many other occurrences like failing to get a promotion. If you should go to a flight room in one of the hangars, you might see a picture of a great big axe over the door and a sign reading, "The Great Hairy Chop." Other common expressions were wizzo, a shaky do, haven't you heard, it's all been changed. There was a serious designation that an airman might be said to have L.M.F. (lack of moral fiber) which could bring serious consequences. I attended medical conferences dealing with the subject but I never did see such a disgraced airman and I would have found it difficult to attach such a label to an eighteen year old boy.

Kirchner: We are at the end of 1942 now?

McNeil: No. This is 1944.

Kirchner: Already '44, before D Day or after?

McNeil: After, in the last months of that year up until VE day in 1945. During this time I took a War Medicine course at Hammersmith Hospital (the postgraduate hospital in London). It was a stimulating course and was given by the best of teachers. This, I remember, was the first time I had heard of the Crush Syndrome, so named because it seemingly was first recognized in air raid casualities, where a victim might be found crushed under a beam and impaled for some hours. It isn't so labelled now and it can, as you know, be brought about in other circumstances, and is termed a Lower Nephron Nephrosis. The pathogenesis of this syndrome is a bit complicated, but it comes as a result of injury to muscle associated with shock, burns, improperly matched blood, drug reactions, etc. The mortality of such a process was high as the mechanisms and management were only beginning to be worked out. We, of course, did not have artifical kidneys to fall back on. It was here that I first heard of the Rh factor in blood which was then designated as blood factors C.D.E. and c.d.e. I have mentioned before the symposium on head injuries which was presented at the same course. I had the opportunity of attending other courses such as a week in a chest hospital, the Fulton Road Hospital in London. These were wonderful opportunities for young physicians, being able to take a course during the day and attend a London theater at night!

FIFTEEN

While I was stationed at Allerton Park in Yorkshire I had my own little "show". A "good show" or a "bad show" was common air force jargon. We had our own ambulance which we would send for as required and it would be supplied with a driver. I soon passed the driving examination of motor transport, which made me more independent. The ambulance was a full sized American Chevrolet having a left hand drive. You will remember that you drive on the left hand side of the road in England and having a vehicle with a left hand drive was a disadvantage. The R.C.A.F. had no hospitals staffed by Canadians as the army did, so it was necessary to transport our patients with more serious problems to civilian hospitals or take them to an R.A.F. hospital twenty or more miles away. I would often drive patients over in the ambulance myself and this would require a couple of hours driving through various little towns and byways. The military hospitals were of high quality and it was worthwhile, too, to attend their ward round and clinics. I recall one of their clinicians telling us that during some of his investigative work he found that his bacterial cultures were contaminated by green mold. He was suggesting to us that the obvious penicillin contamination might have been discovered by himself, had he appreciated the significance of the observation. Penicillin, the antibiotic, was important news then, and was soon to be made available.

One of you gentlemen asked me when I first remembered using penicillin. This is very clear in my mind. A small amount was made available to us and we had specific directions as to how it should be used. At my unit, it was to be administered for the treatment of VD in air crew only and principally to pilots. My first supply was a bottle of 100,000 units of this brown powder (penicillin is now pure white). My first patient was a young Canadian pilot who had done at least one bombing tour and possessed this easygoing, carefree personality so suited to this career. The dose to be administred was 100,000 units given as 20,000 units for five doses. Should this treatment not be successful, we were directed to send the patient to the south of England to a VD hospital. When the treatment was not quite successful, I arranged for the transfer, taking him away from his duties. Now, of course, one would use five or ten million units of the purified penicillin for such a problem. Following this, penicillin became abundant fairly

78

rapidly. The antibiotic had been discovered in Britain, but the manufacturing process was developed and carried out in the U.S.A. I would like to tell you a story revolving around this same officer of whom I have just spoken.

Kirchner: Please, go ahead.

McNeil: Sometimes we received distinguished visitors; Churchill or other VIPs would visit us, even royalty. We were told that the Princess Royal (the King's oldest sister) would make a tour of the station. We were advised that all areas should look their best, but that I should not be too concerned as she would not likely inspect the station hospital. During her visit I was sitting quietly in my office with my feet on the desk, when the nursing sister came to tell me that the Royal visitor was here and in the women's ward. This sudden appearance made me feel very flustered. I arrived properly dressed at the other side of the hospital, meeting the group of people with her. To my great embarrassment, I saluted her Lady-in-Waiting rather than the princess. She tried to be as friendly and relaxed with me as possible and graciously asked me to accompany her around the wards. We walked around the large general wards, then entered one or two of the private rooms. Here, in one of these rooms was the R.C.A.F. officer, the one with V.D. My embarrassment became complete when the Princess asked me the nature of the officer's illness. I couldn't find any suitable words and my distress was intensified when the patient, in an inquisitive but charming way, mischievously encouraged me to answer her.

Kirchner: Were you directed to uncover the source of VD, if possible?

McNeil: Yes, there was a VD protocol, and we were supposed to complete this carefully. I think we were more successful in this regard in Canada. A R.C.A.F. VD control officer visited us regularly to examine our documents. Certain cities like the large city of Leeds nearby were "out of bounds" to other ranks (not officers) because of the incidence of venereal disease.

Kirchner: Were you required to stay in England following the conclusion of the war in Europe?

McNeil: Yes, I was. There was great need for military services for a long time. Our aircraft were still flying, bringing servicemen back from the continent and carrying out a number of duties. The aircrew often possessed a yellow color to their skin, the result of the malaria prophylaxis drugs, because they were flying to the Middle East and further. I was stationed for a period at the large bomber base at Leamington in Yorkshire, where I saw a few of the inmates of the German concentration camps. These people, lying on stretchers, unable to speak or move, looked more dead than alive.

While I did not have the opportunity to join a fighter squadron, and therefore see Europe, I did have a remarkable opportunity to fly over many of the great German and Dutch cities which had been bombed. This flight in a Lancaster took place about a day or two after VE day. We flew at low levels and had the opportunity to see the devastation. On a later visit to Cologne, Mary Lou and I were told that the Cathedral had not been damaged during the war! On the day that I flew over that city, the only building standing was the Cathedral, but its interior, at the low level we were flying, we could see had been gutted.

Kirchner: Was your wife at that time in Canada, or was she with you?

McNeil: Mary Lou was in Canada.

Kirchner: Most likely very anxious for her husband.

McNeil: She was busy taking care of our first daughter. We were most anxious to have a family but it was rather a surprise to learn of this pregnancy around the time that I was posted overseas. Susan was two years old before I was able to see her. Mary Lou had a most difficult time with the pregnancy like so many other service wives who were without their husbands. The Clinic doctors took great care of her. I lost my father when I was over there. The cables for both of these events were not received for at least a week after the event. I remember VE and VJ days very well. I was on the station on VE day — the celebrations for that day were not great as the announcement had been expected for some time. I was in London for VJ day, and the city was chaotic! I joined the crowds in front of Buckingham Palace to see and hear the King and Queen. The relief that could be seen in the faces of the civilian people was very evident. On trains almost anywhere, after this they would spontaneously burst out into song.

Kirchner: Euphoria?

McNeil: Yes, you could see that this terrible burden, the breakup of homes, the absent family members, and all that war had meant was now, after so long, really lifted.

Kirchner: What I don't see clearly when you were serving overseas, were you part of a Canadian unit which could be identified or rather were you integrated into the RAF?

McNeil: The Canadians were largely integrated. The RAF was made up of British, Canadian, Australian, New Zealander, and other Commonwealth personnel. People in Canada raised the same question you have asked. They complained that in reports of action, it was the RAF which seemed to singularly carry out a raid. They knew that Canadians were involved as indicated by the casualty lists, etc., but press referred only to the R.A.F. One effort to correct this was the formation of an entire Canadian bomber group, the No. 6, to which I was attached. Bomber Command (all of the groups) was comprised of airmen from every Commonwealth country, but one's own country was indicated by a shoulder flash.

Kirchner: You have mentioned other places, such as Leamington, where you were stationed. Please tell us about this or other situations you experienced.

McNeil: After VE day, Allerton Park and the castle was gradually closed down and these weeks were very pleasant. With minimal duties to perform and glorious weather, we went on leave, cycled around the countryside, played golf, or joined the Air Commodore and a few of the remaining officers touring the north of England in his limousine. I had one more posting in the area to a large base at Leamington in Yorkshire. This was a permanent R.A.F. base and I had the luxury of living in a suite provided for my own use. There were large numbers of service people here and their planes were still flying regularly. A W.A.A.F. (women's service) appeared on sick parade one day and I found her to be in the late stages of labour. The medical staff had noted her appearance before but had been reassured by the W.A.A.F. officers that her appearance was a peculiar bodily stature! Pregnancy occurred frequently as you would realize. Many of the service women married while in the forces. For the unmarried, the instructions to medical officers were clear — in addition to carrying out a medical board for the discharge and arranging for their repatriation we should show every consideration to these women. Abortion was not offered and I found it very difficult to be encouraging to the girls as they countenanced returning to their homes and families. I was transferred from Leamington to RCAF Overseas Headquarters in London.

I became the medical officer to this central Canadian Air Force Headquarters. Rather like No. 6 Group at Allerton Park I was in charge of this unit with my own staff, and like Allerton Park my patients were senior air force officers and their technicians and assistants. I have wondered at times why I was chosen for these particular jobs — — was it a compliment or otherwise? I had no hospital or sick quarter beds here and those requiring admission were sent to Canadian Army Hospitals in the vicinity of London. There were no air force living arrangements in London, so I lived, at first, in a fourth or fifth storey room in Earl's Court. As I tried to carry on some serious study, I would be wrapped in a blanket and would damn the gas heater as it would shut down, requiring another shilling. I was fortunate, eventually, to have my application accepted at London House. This building in Russell Square was and remains a residence for commonwealth scholars studying in Britain. Perhaps you have heard of it? The quarters were pleasant, the library heated, and some books were available. My roommate, a naval officer and a South African, was another of those fine men I have had the privilege of meeting in my life. When I inquired about the reason for the many bruises on this "true gentleman's" body, I learned that he was still a championship boxer of the London medical schools, and a noted boxer for England. I made several excursions with him to his medical school, Guy's Hospital, to Brighton for a weekend with his in-laws, and to a rugger game in London. At the rugger game I was to learn that he had a reputation in this sport, too, and shared (at half time) with the team a visit by the King who was in attendance with the Queen in this rather small stadium. There were certain receptions held at London House and at one of these while visiting with Viscount Bennett, (the former Prime Minister of Canada, R.B. Bennett formerly of Calgary) I was introduced to Air Marshall Tedder, Marshall of the Royal Air Force.

Many of us took the opportunity for extra study while in the U.K. Some of the men actually earned higher degrees such as a F.R.C.P. (Eng). I attended such clinics as the one presided over by Dr. Parkinson, the noted cardiologist. Dr. Parkinson had associated himself with Drs. White and Wolff, the American cardiologists, and reported the heart conduction abnormality, the W.P.W. syndrome. These clinics were held at various hospitals, and meetings of The London Medical Surgical Society were enjoyed for most of the year that I was stationed at Lincoln's Inn Field. I met students from many of the commonwealth countries while I continued living at London House.

Kirchner: This was a type of leave of absence from the service?

McNeil: No, this was while I was still in uniform and working. Service responsibilities were minimal and on an ordinary day I could finish my work in a couple of hours. Life was harder for our wives at home that it was for us, I must admit.

Kirchner: So you had the freedom to read, leave the hospital, and go out?

McNeil: As a medical officer you had considerable liberty. Indeed, much earlier than this, a Bomber Command signal had advised all commanding officers that they would be unwise to interfere in the movement of medical officers in any manner. I believe that the directive was worded in that manner. This liberty included transportation, how he used his ambulance, etc. At the conclusion of the war and while I was still in Yorkshire, I had little or no difficulty in obtaining an aircraft to travel anywhere. I flew to Glasgow in a large two engine plane as the only passenger and the purpose of the flight was my leave in Scotland. Railway transportation was readily available from one's own unit. I had a splendid leave; a week in Paris and all of the costs of transportation and billeting were provided by the air force. One other officer and myself had our own guide (a beautiful Parisienne lady . . . a city volunteer) to show us the city. During the time in Paris I visited the Pasteur Institute along with doing all the touristy things. The staging barracks at Calais were something else in that wrecked city; but realizing the thousand of troops who would have preceded me passing through the unit, the fact the beds had no mattresses could be understood.

Some think that the deportment and behavior of Canadian

servicemen was better than that of our colleagues in the Amercian services. I don't think this was so. They had just as much money, and could be arrogant and overbearing. They did not consider themselves as colonials, and similarly could demonstrate their own poor taste. The British service personnel had low incomes, and a sign which might be seen on a military convey stating "Don't wave, girls, we're British" might reflect this state of affairs. Military men of both nations were healthy, strong, and therefore, more gregarious. This was evidenced by the VD rates which were higher than those of other nations, including the French, who are often regarded as the most sex orientated.

SIXTEEN

All this had to end and I was eventually issued my repatriation orders. We sailed from Southampton on the former French liner, the Ile de France. I didn't think then that this ship would ever go back into service again as a luxury liner. It had been used as a troopship and the French were said to have complained of the damage the ship received. It was a most pleasant voyage not only because we were on the way home, but now there were no restrictions as to movement as had existed on the Mauritania on the way over. On board were hundreds of war brides and they, as I remember, were a flirtatious group, and seemingly quite inclined to strike up a shipboard romance.

Kirchner: It will be interesting to tell us of your reactions upon returning home.

McNeil: There were few signs of a war in Canada; uniforms were disappearing and much industrial activity was apparent; no food or clothes rationing existed, which was still present in England. For my first meal I had a T bone steak followed immediately by a second one at a restaurant in Montreal. The ambience was entirely different to Europe as seen in the street, the stores, and in people's faces. I travelled by train to meet the family in Winnipeg. The press was there to meet the train and in the newspapers they reported to my embarrassment things I did not say. Mary Lou was beautiful as was the little girl she held up to me — the daughter whom I had not seen before and who would have nothing to do with this stranger. Of course Dad was not there, but mother and the boys with their wives made the homecoming so wonderful. After a few days with mother and the family, Mary Lou, Susan, and I returned to Calgary. One did not expect to be treated like a hero, but having recently left Europe and their problems, and now meeting people whose interests were personal or selfish made it a difficult adjustment.

Kirchner: Your war service was quickly forgotten?

McNeil: My military service endeavor was naturally of little consequence. The apartment we rented was menial and others complained of the presence of the little girl. On visiting the clinic after the initial welcome, one realized there were a number of changes. Many new men had arrived and were now firmly established. These men and women had been able to complete graduate training while others were

84

still in Europe in the Service. I was a stranger, of course, to the new doctors who had arrived and they were busy establishing their own practices.

I had no intention of returning to the Clinic until I had my qualifications in Internal Medicine. There were no residencies available in Canada or the States. The positions had all been filled by doctors who had been discharged earlier. I found a course available to me at McGill University in Montreal. This was about three months in length, with lectures and clinics given by the best clinicians of the faculty. It was a matter of saying goodbye to my little family again and heading east. We were separated for several months; during the course I lived at the "Y" and studied intensely.

This course, entitled "F.R.C.P. Preparation", gave us, in addition to a superior overview of the whole of internal medicine, the first gratuitous feeling I would experience upon my return to Canada. I found that McGill teachers demonstrated a sincere desire to help us to make up for lost time. The course covered cardiology, neurology, hematology, nephrology, gastroenterology, etc. We were given excellent reviews of importance in these basic subjects. We spent many hours in pathology and Dr. Beck (the pathologist) was an authority on Collagen disease, a subject receiving a great deal of attention at that time. Dr. Meakin was the Dean of Medicine at McGill and his presence was felt along with other good men. I would like to mention one of these in particular, namely, Dr. Walter Scriver, who was in charge of the course. He watched our progress most carefully. We were required to complete a medical examination each week and through this he was able to assess our ability. There were two types of qualifications that you might seek in your specialty, the lesser of the two, "Certification" or the more prestigious one, "Fellowship in the Royal College". I had decided that I would attempt the lesser qualification and was humble about my chances of obtaining this degree. Dr. Scriver, upon learning of my choice, made every effort to convince me that I was entirely capable of successfully passing the fellowship. I want to add that I had another great supporter in this regard and that was Mary Lou, who had now joined me in Montreal before examinations.

To have the privilege of sitting for these examinations, one had to provide evidence of approved training as is required today. While one was given credits for military service, previous practice, and in my case, the association with Dr. Scarlett, I am certain that the courses and studies I took advantage of in Britain were of considerable importance. I listed them all in my application. My son had six years of graduate training before he attempted the fellowship examinations. I was now 35 years of age with a family and knew it was incumbent upon me to establish a practice at home soon. I was treated, I thought, generously by the Royal College with regard to their assessment of my credentials.

I developed a respect for the Royal College and for people like Dr. Scriver who were so supportive. I, or rather Mary Lou, had saved money from my military service income which had been carefully laid aside. These funds were in the form of war bonds and were gradually dissipated as we lived in Montreal for the following year. Should I have failed the fellowship that autumn it would have been difficult to financially prepare for a later examination. Other than Mary Lou and Dr. Scriver, there was one other person who influenced me to make the step. I ran into Don Wilson of Edmonton at McGill, who later became professor of medicine in Alberta. Don and I have been friends for many years. He, too, had recently been discharged from the service and was doing some graduate work, I believe, in Boston. He was in Montreal for the purpose of sitting for the F.R.C.P. tests. He encouraged me to write the examination. I told him I didn't have time to do two or three years residency training even if it were available. I had to get to work since I had a family and a home to take care of.

To shorten this story, having returned from Europe in March of that year, by September I possessed the degree. I cannot remember that I had very much difficulty with the long written papers. I had no problems with the bedside orals but did falter a little over one or two of the old specimens in the pathology oral.

Kirchner: The qualifications you sought were for the specialty of Internal Medicine?

McNeil: Yes, Internal Medicine. Although I had my degree, and was therefore fully qualified as a specialist, I hesitated about beginning specialty practice immediately. You will remember that, as with my original M.D. degree, I hesitated to enter General Practice without further training! I obtained a fellowship, or perhaps better described as a loose association, with Dr. D. J. Kaufman in the department of hematology at the Royal Victoria Hospital which was to last for the next six months.

Kirchner: In Montreal?

McNeil: Yes, at the Royal Victoria Hospital which is situated adjacent to McGill University. I learned quite a lot of valuable medicine with Dr. D. J. Kaufman. He was a noted hematologist and I returned to Calgary with expertise not previously available in this field. The arrangement I had in the hematology department was in some regards superior to that of a residency: I was free to take part in any other educational activity going on in the hospital as I had almost no regular duties. We lived in a temporary family residence at McGill. It consisted of several buildings: barracks which were taken over from the air force at Lachine, the same overseas staging unit that I have mentioned before. It was provided for students and their families who had been in the service and was a type of communal living which was fine for a limited time.

Kirchner: Having spent, I think, almost a year in Montreal, you then returned to Calgary. Tell us about your thoughts then.

McNeil: I completed a year in Montreal. The military service educational gratuities (of about one hundred and fifty dollars a month), provided by the Department of Veteran's Affairs, were available for the same number of months as the term of your military service. Mine would have lasted four years and so these were not exhausted, but I had had enough of studying by then. Further, our savings were now entirely gone and we did want to establish our home. Driving west we stopped in Winnipeg, and I was invited by my old friend and senior medical officer from MacLeod to join his group The Mall Medical Clinic. This would have been fine but Dr. Scarlett and the Associate Clinic had indicated their interest in my return. They had published my picture in the local newpaper reporting my return to specialty work and had the usual congratulatory communications from many of the group.

Kirchner: So, in fact, you were considered sort of a family member of the Clinic now.

McNeil: I suppose that could be said.

Kirchner: You returned to Calgary in the spring of '47?

McNeil: I was now almost 35 years of age and without any assets other than my medical degrees. We had no home and it was almost impossible to get one. I borrowed a hundred dollars from the Clinic and sent Mary Lou and Susan to her parents until I could obtain one. I made quite an effort to get a house including an interview with the mayor, to whom I suggested that I might not remain in the city should I not obtain accommodation for my family. We eventually obtained a nice little wartime house not too far from here. I was now to experience the Associate Clinic, a much larger and changed place from that which I left in the early stages of the war.

Kircher: What was the most important contribution of the Calgary Associate Clinic to the people of Calgary?

McNeil: The Clinic, I think, deserves recognition at least for this one contribution: they brought highly qualified physicians to the city much like a medical school does, a long time before the medical school was envisioned. They lost their goal of being a recognized referral centre when they tried to be both a family practice and a referral specialty centre. Referring doctors did not accept the combination of specialists and general practitioners. Also, a central location for family practice became impractical.

Kirchner: I am curious about the proceedings and nature of the Clinic meetings. I am somewhat familiar, as you know, with the publications of the Historical Society of the Calgary Associate Clinic. I think that I have the volumes comprising all that was printed. I would be interested in any of your recollections of this and of other meetings which were generated by the group.

McNeil: There were several types of meetings as you suggest. The library was the focal point for many of these, be it for the afternoon coffee break or the various scheduled formal meetings. The library was used a great deal by doctors in and outside the office for several reasons. We subscribed to a broad cross-section of medical journals, and the central location of the library made these and our other books readily available. We employed a full-time librarian, one carefully chosen for her ability in this regard by Dr. Scarlett. Dr. Scarlett was instrumental in much of the library activity, but others like Dr. Stanley and Dr. Price contributed as well. It was called the Dr. G. D. Stanley library and the large brass name plate, from his original office in High River, hung over the door. The regular group meeting, "the Wednesday noon luncheon" (convened almost always in the Spanish Room of the Palliser Hotel) was an institution. We would enjoy a full lunch while we listened to a program. Occasionally the speaker would be a guest, but the speaker was usually a Clinic doctor. One of us would have attended a recent meeting or convention and he or she would be expected to share some of the learning. Failing this, one of us would present a paper to which he would have given some care and attention. We did have occasional combined evening meetings with our wives and I can remember one with the presence of a Jewish Rabbi telling us a little about Hebrew philosophy and customs. Another was on art appreciation, and given, I think, by Illingsworth Kerr, the local artist of note. The meetings of the Historical Society evoked the broadest interest and will possibly be the most notable legacy of the Associate Clinic. The Historical Society commenced, as I remember, as little private meetings held in the evenings in the old library in the basement of the office. The speakers, at first, were Clinic members and it was only much later when invited speakers were heard. I gave one back in 1941 and I remember the attention I enjoyed while I presented my subject: the influence on history of the illness of Henry the Eighth.

Dr. Scarlett's interest in the history of medicine was eclectic, ranging from the ancient to recent times. This was shown by the selections and invitations to pioneer doctors to tell their stories, be it about Grand Prairie, the Peace River, Lethbridge, or Medicine Hat. I think allowance for the expenses incurred by these men was offered, but I do not know whether the offering was ever accepted. Any cost for the operation of the society was borne by the Clinic, of course.

Kirchner: This idea came from Dr. Scarlett to invite these gentlemen and was he the instigator of activities?

McNeil: He was the principal motivator for all of this. I have given credit already to two of the other men, who were more active supporters,

88

but I would like to say all the members took pride in the endeavor and all gave their tacit support.

Kirchner: In respect to Dr. Scarlett, a man so preoccupied with other things than strictly medical care, how was he able to provide a decent service to his patients?

McNeil: To answer this would require a knowledge and description of his character and personality. His original training was excellent; his appreciation for continuing education was fulfilled by reading medical literature, by keeping close contact with medial centres through personal correspondence, and by this frequent attendance at major scientific meetings. He accomplished this, notwithstanding that he was far removed from the principal centres. Dr. Macnab told me that it was to their amazement that they could attract Dr. Scarlett to Calgary from his teaching position at the University of Iowa. His ability was always evident and his reputation in the profession was maintained throughout his life. To quote the editor of Dr. Scarlett's book, *In Sickness and in Health*, "Sparkled by humor and by deep love for his colleagues, his profession and people in general his book reaffirms faith in human honor, dignity, and meaning." This provides somewhat of an assessment of him. He was a disciplined man in all that he did. A certain amount of time was set aside for every activity he engaged in, be it a consultation, a letter, writing, music, or time with his family. In his book there is a quote from Praxithea to her son Hippocrates who is in love with Daphne. "Hippocrates . . . Don't always be a physician! Daphne is a woman not a patient, not a horse . . . the help you need is the help a wife could give you. Through her you would learn the other half of life. Without her you may be only half a man. Your father used to say, Nothing in excess! Too much medicine . . . too much work even . . . too much kindly service may be excessive." In regard to the last quote, Mrs. Scarlett was the perfect doctor's wife, and he did acknowledge her contribution at every opportunity. I knew her well as I became the physician to the family, caring for her through at least one coronary occlusion. I also cared for Dr. Scarlett when he had several episodes of the same disease. His failings did become apparent at times; for, as I have said, his time was compartmentalized. You would realize that as new or additional problems appeared they must always be fitted into that one compartment, and therefore the attention given to any one consultation might become short indeed. In such circumstances any of us can fail as he occasionally did. I, on the other hand, lacked most of the qualities that he possessed; I have almost never been on time; every task that I undertook required longer than expected; a new request for service required that much more time. I arrived late at the office; I left the office late at night, arrived home late for supper so much so that Mary Lou said, "You are missing all the fun with the kids." Before I destroy myself entirely, I would like to say that my son became a doctor and my other children followed somewhat similar lives and sought higher education. Dr. Scarlett could understand even one such as I. In a book given to me after my attendance at an illness of his or Mrs. Scarlett's, he inscribed, "To one who has been friend, comrade, physician, and who has carried on the tradition of a noble company of associates, who at all times and to all persons quietly exercising the ancient art . . . With grateful thanks . . . signed Earle Scarlett." It would be appropriate for Dr. Scarlett that this gift book deals with the history of medicine. It is *The Epic of Medicine* and is written by his friend Dr. Felix Marti Ibanez, whom, as you know, was the editor of the journal M.D. which still carries on, relating the history of medicine today. To tell you a little more about Dr. Scarlett, I would add that he was born in Manitoba and raised in a Clergyman's home there. He enlisted and served as a machine gunner on the western front in World War One where he was seriously wounded. I recall one of those many "pearls" he has given me over numerous encounters: I wakened in this field hospital after I was wounded and there was my chaplain father standing at my beside, and by way of introducing his companion, said . . . Earle, this is Dr. Harvey Cushing whom I would like you to meet." Dr. Scarlett's love of literature provided him with his first work as a junior professor at Wesley College in Winnipeg. His interest in travel perhaps was stimulated by his work as a C.P.R. conductor of sleeping cars during the summer. His love for music brought the first hi-fi system to Calgary and the musical evenings we would all attend at his home. With the culmination of the evening by the playing of Bach he would state solemnly, as he turned off the machine, that no music of any kind must be played after Bach! I hope you will find these observations of interest and pertinent to your question in relation to this truly great man.

SEVENTEEN

Kirchner: Would you summarize Dr. Scarlett's activities, which I know were many in number, and then I would like to ask you a question which, I think, would naturally follow your reply.

McNeil: I have already referred to his professional activity; his attention to patients in consultation and the many he saw on a private or personal basis. He carried on private correspondence with friends dealing with philosophical, historical, and medical subjects. As an author he regularly contributed editorials to the Archives of Internal Medicine, and occasionally contributed to a number of other publications under the caption, "Gleanings from the Common Place Book of a Medical Reader". As you know many titles in our Historical Bulletin are under his name; he was the writer of at least one book, *In Sickness and in Health*. He was active in musical circles in the city and he was the senior consultant at a local Veterans Hospital. He became the Chancellor of the University of Alberta as well as the president of the Associate Clinic. An ardent devotee of Sherlock Holmes, he was an active member of the "Baker Street Irregulars" and a member of a number of societies both medical and otherwise. I cannot say whether he supported a church, although he was the son of a minister. He did have a faith, for in the last paragraph of his book he quotes a man whose philosophy he could support: "The groping towards a power beyond the things of sense may be too vague to put into the form of a dogma or creed. That matters less. What does matter is that the human mind is not confined to the things that today are here and tomorrow are gone. What does matter is the sense of the eternal informs our doing and our thinking, that the horizon does not limit our vision . . . we rest in the assurance that underneath are the everlasting arms." He did recommend the reading of the New Testament to me and I understood that advice as representing a basic educational admonition.

Kirchner: Did he have a confidant who would replace him when he went away for conferences and meetings and who would take care of his patients?

McNeil: I think the Associate Clinic was rather ideal for him. There were always one or two of the internists ready to do his work. This would include the care of those patients who were in the hospital and those of his private practice. At times we thought the burden was heavy, but he would have made every effort to have attended all perceived eventualities.

Kirchner: Who were the others?

McNeil: This gives me the opportunity to mention several of my friends. Dr. Thorson, who has carried on a distinguished practice in Calgary, was a member of the Clinic for a period, and it was the interest of the Clinic which brought him to the city. A Dr. Houghtling was his associate during the war and Dr. Desmond Muldoon came a little later in the fifties. Dr. Muldoon, a kind person, (the Irish — particularly Irish literary men, always favorites of Dr. Scarlett) was at all times ready to attend his own multitude of patients plus those of the other internists. I would mention Dr. Tom Golding who later moved to Florida as another of the active internists of this period.

One of Dr. Scarlett's weaknesses was his inability to appreciate the economic aspects of his own practice. To illustrate this . . . I remember an extremely wealthy man, Dr. Scarlett's patient, who was a patient in the hospital for several weeks. The problem of this grave illness necessitated a great deal of attention, and I, by chance, found out later that the complete charge submitted to the patient was the large sum of thirty five dollars. I could understand it when I later learned that his earnings were insufficient to provide for his own income. It is important for the observer of the Clinic to know that very little of the economic affairs (such as the earnings of oneself or your colleagues) was known to members, including partners. I'm sure that you will see a fairly lofty virtue to this situation. This might be an example for later times where the first concern of the doctor does not always seem to be the medical aspects of the problem or the welfare of the patient. An incident comes to mind which is worthy of relating . . . I think of the shame the partners all felt when at a meeting chaired by Dr. Scarlett in which he imparted the disgrace he felt at the contribution we as a group had made to the recent drive of the Community Chest. I believe we immediately reassessed our charitable responsibility and acted accordingly.

Kirchner: I think we have discussed quite a lot about Dr. Scarlett. It would be interesting now to hear your own recollections of when you were at the Clinic.

McNeil: Prior to my return to Calgary my picture (in uniform) was shown in the local paper with the announcement that this physician would rejoin the Clinic after service and study. Having been honored, with the Royal College Fellowship I would possess the qualifications of a specialist.

Kirchner: The Calgary Herald?

McNeil: Yes, the Calgary Herald . . . I may have been so vain as to have saved a copy of the page. Such an announcement is, of course, quite proper, but the College of Physicians and Surgeons and the Canadian Medical Association require certain proprieties. In making a submission to the press one must avoid imparting any impression of unprofessional advertising. To begin my work in internal medicine it was necessary to provide credentials to the College of Physicians and to the appropriate hospital staff committees. I believe I was the first man now in Calgary who had earned Fellowship qualifications by examination. There were several doctors who had an F.R.C.P., and like Dr. Scarlett, they were charter members of the college receiving the degree adeundum. The Calgary General Hospital provided me with courtesy privileges as was the custom for all new members. These courtesy privileges would be mandatory for one year notwithstanding that I had been a member of the staff before I had enlisted. However, this courtesy arrangement did not last very long because they approached me within a very few weeks requesting that I accept the position as the Chief of the Department of Medicine. The obvious explanation for this change in my status was the necessity now for the hospital to meet the requirements for their hospital accreditation. All accreditation was under the jurisdiction of the American College of Surgeons. The accreditation examiners reviewed the qualifications of all staff, but it was essential that suitable evidence of competency of its heads of departments be shown. The General Hospital had for years been dominated by a small group of physicians who resisted change and whose work did not always permit scrutiny. This was made abundantly clear to my good friend Dr. Howard McEwen, when after admission to the staff, he was appointed to the chairmanship of the audit committee. He, while carrying out the duties in a responsible manner, submitted his first report, as was required by accreditation. The reaction of senior physicians of the hospital was prompt, and he was advised that he cease this intrusion into private matters. While retaining his position of the chairman of the committee, he would do so without reference to medical records!

Kirchner: These men were administrators or physicians?

McNeil: These were practicing physicians and they had a tremendous influence at the hospital. There was no medical administration in either hospital at first. At the Holy Cross the Sister Superior and her sisters were the administrators. The General Hospital was essentially under the direction of the city council and the hospital was required to conform to political influences, and to vocal admonitions of self-seeking aldermen. Remuneration for appointed heads of departments or other offices was a late development and did not occur during my period in these positions. The Holy Cross was influenced by the two large Clinics and generally had a moderate number of physicians with higher qualifications. The General Hospital had a lesser number of specialty qualified physicians. I was the Chief of Medicine at the General for

93

some years but had little time, and little support, to carry out the duties properly. The hospitals did improve slowly, as new, young, and well trained doctors arrived with determination to bring about changes.

Kirchner: I would like to ask you about the religious groups and their interest in the hospitals. You have referred to them often.

McNeil: When I was in Winnipeg, my junior internship was taken at a Sisters' Hospital, the St. Boniface Hospital. This and the Holy Cross were owned and operated by The Sisters of Charity and so my career has always been associated with these Catholic hospitals. The story of their founder Marguerite D'Youville and the development of the sisterhood in the eighteenth century in Montreal is contained briefly but nobly in a brochure entitled *Love at Work* which is in part written by my friend Sister Cecilia Leclerc. Perhaps you will accept this brochure as an addition to your special library collection. The sisterhood now numbers some 7,000 members with five autonomous branches and operates charitable hospitals over most of the continent. The early history was very different and to quote from the brochure, "Disapproval by the clergy, protests from the aristocracy, the Sisters of Charity did not judge their detractors. They continued their work among the needy and with humility cherished the old name Les Soeurs Grises — The Grey Nuns." The story of the Holy Cross and the four nuns who pioneered its origin in the 1890's is chronicled by Mr. Jack Peach, whom I think I have referred to.

I came to know the Sisters very well in various ways: as my nursing colleagues, as the administrators of the hospital, through many committees, often as their physician, sometimes as a private counselor as they endeavored to manage or sort out problems, and sometimes as their teacher when a Sister would be a student nurse. The background of the Sisters, as I knew them, varied tremendously. Some came from poorer homes where they could not have the benefit of higher education. Many, however, were highly educated possessing university degrees. Their personalities differed as you would expect and whereas I developed a great regard and a deep respect for the Sisters, there were the occasional nuns who were difficult to appreciate. They were always faithful to their vows of humility and charity. We still happily keep in contact with some of the Sisters. A number of the order can be included in that group of mine, the "special people" I have encountered in my life.

Kirchner: Were they running the hospital? That is, did they fill the position of the administrator?

McNeil: Yes. They were obliged to operate in the most economical manner possible as the fiscal responsibility was their own. They could not fall back upon government or other resources. The cost of administration and many other duties was minimal. The nursing school provided an economic advantage in that the educational cost was the responsibility of the student through her service. There was very little waste in material or equipment such as exists today. Supplies such as linens were repaired rather than being discarded. Economy in the provision of food services earned a poor reputation for the meals in the hospital. As an intern at the Holy I could support such a position. The General Hospital, on the other hand, had an excellent reputation in this regard, perhaps as the result of their greater government resources. Economy in health services is not politically in vogue now, as frugality in health care could be related to infringement on people's rights.

My position at the Holy Cross while being somewhat unique, was, I think, of mutual benefit. I hope you will see me as one who enjoyed a position of earned trust and not one who simply took advantage of opportunities. I often was acknowledged as the Sisters' doctor, and as such had the uncustomary privilege of being permitted to enter their community. As an example of their generosity towards me I would like to tell you one or two stories. Mary Lou, during her fifth pregnancy, became critically ill. She developed a Miliary Tuberculosis, the old so called "Galloping Consumption", from which she would have died had not the effective antibiotics become recently available. We now had four children, the oldest aged ten: My practice was extremely demanding and you would appreciate the problems we faced. Many friends, including my colleagues, Mary Lou's family and mine, gave us great support, but the sisters rallied to our needs beyond measure.

Although this extremely infectious disease was not ordinarily handled in a general hospital, she remained at the Holy for some weeks and was shown all kindness, without any pressure for us to hurry her transfer to the Baker Sanatorium. Over at least the next year of the illness they found innumerable ways to express their thoughtfulness and their kindness to us. On many occasions then and later, the six of us on returning from church (Knox United) Sunday morning would enjoy a beautifully prepared dinner set in a private dining room at the Holy Cross. I could continue to give you many examples of their generosity. The assistant Sister Superior, Sister Leona Breux, had occupied several senior positions in the Grey Nuns hospitals before coming to Calgary, but because of illness had assumed a lesser position at the Holy Cross. She became of considerable significance in my medical life. She possessed a great deal of knowledge in the management of hospitals, and what is more she possessed great intelligence and a strong determined personality. Her influence in the hospital was widely felt. For example, while examining the qualifications of doctors on staff, she found that the Chief of Medicine had been in that position for a long time. Sister Breux, with her usual determination, apparently found that my qualifications were entirely adequate and I found myself one day the Head of the Department of Medicine. She suffered from an illness not adequately diagnosed before coming to Calgary, and I had occasion to watch at her bedside through several crises of this eventually fatal illness. I could tell you of many other examples of sisters who stand out in my estimation as epitomizing the highest qualities of the nursing profession but any such attempt by me to do this would only be inadequate. To mention just two, I think of Sister Cecilia Leclerc, the Director of Nursing and Sister Luciene Garneau, in charge of the Operating Room. They carried out their work with wisdom and kindness in the interest of both the patients and the doctors. I think of the latter sister at a time much earlier, perhaps in 1941, when I was confronted with a problem. This was situated around a very poor family, all of them suffering from a severe enteric infection. I arranged for the admission of several of the most ill to hospital, but the sister, recognizing my concern for the rest of the family encouraged me to bring in the whole family, and so we filled more than two four-bed wards with one family.

Good nursing care was by no means limited to the Holy Cross. I have spoken of this previously but would like to acknowledge the generally excellent nursing services available at the General Hospital too. This was provided by the high quality of the student nurses and their training program as directed early on by Miss Hebert, the director of nursing (whom I cared for medically up until her passing). I would particularly like to mention such nurses as Miss Mary Hooper, Miss Von Grunigen, and the wonderful Miss Margaret McDonald, "Black Mac", whom I have mentioned before. She was paid a very suitable tribute, written by one of her students, namely Margorie Hughes, and is contained in a letter to the Herald of January 6, 1977. Miss Eileen Jamieson, later a Director of Nursing, served the hospital and the community with great devotion for many years. I must mention Mrs. Henry, in charge of nursing education for a long time, and Miss Longmore, the charge nurse on West Five who made many contributions to the development of the General Hospital Diabetic Service. I joined Dr. Howard McEwen and Dr. Steve Thorson in this project. This work established a model of monitored uniform care for the diabetic in an "open" hospital. The methodology and the report of the studies demonstrating the resulting improvement in patient care was published. The work and the people involved have received recognition. No reference to the hospital would be complete without some acknowledgement of Miss Gertrude Hall. Miss Hall, as the director of the nursing school was appreciated across the country as the avant-courier of modern nursing education. This warm person was loved by her students, and passed away suddenly at the conclusion of a nursing graduation ceremony. She was supported in her work by a nurse of similar qualities, Miss Margaret Street. I consider it a privilege that I gave some medical lectures to the General Hospital nurses.

With further regard to the religious involvement in hospitals, the Salvation Army must always be recognized. They have maintained large hospitals in many Canadian centres such as Winnipeg. They did have some connection with the original Children's Hospital in Calgary and they continue to operate the Grace Hospital in the city. I have had the opportunity to know a number of their officers. The veterans of the two great wars such as Mary Lou's father and myself have reason to praise that organization. The Lutheran Church continues to operate a very fine auxiliary hospital, the Bethany Care Centre. The Jewish people maintain hospitals such as the Jewish General Hospital in Montreal. The United Church of Canada has had some hospital ventures elsewhere, but I do not think that they had any particular operation in Calgary. They have been influential in political lobbying pertaining to medical insurance legislation.

Kirchner: What was the reason that the religious order somehow gradually became driven out of administration?

McNeil: This did not happen until after the acceptance of the report of the Royal Commission on Health Services. The commission recommended that government assume the total responsibility for the provision of health services. The sisters sold their hospital to the Provincial Government and took the money to use for their other charities. Of course, there remain large Sisters' hospitals, but they are controlled and funded by government.

Kirchner: This occurred when you were still in practice?

McNeil: Yes, it did.

Kirchner: Did you notice any sort of anger from the Sisters when this happened? If not anger, then a disappointment?

McNeil: Some of the changes were gradual; the Sisters became less visible as they were transferred elsewhere or moved back East. I do not really think they were capable of anger as all through their long history they were forced to accommodate to vicissitudes and change. I would expect that they would have been disappointed. I cannot remember that there was any public celebration of recognition for their contributions to Calgary over all these years. The Church and charitable organizations have largely moved out of medical care as charity seems to be an anathema to social programs. It is, as you know, an established tenet that the government will do it all.

Kirchner: You have spoken of the nursing training schools, expressing your admiration for their programs. When Foothills Hospital was created, they founded another one, the Foothills Nursing School. Was it also founded by the Sisters?

McNeil: The Foothills Hospital is a provincial government institution and it has its own board of directors. The board would have appointed the Nursing Director. The selection of Mrs. Troningsdal was very appropriate and she was highly regarded. She was very successful as the director during those first years of the school and up until her retirement. I was invited to arrange the medical courses and examinations for the first class. I requested that Dr. Don Wallace and Dr. John Dawson assist me. I was impressed in that exercise by the use of the "Minnesota Multiphasic Personality Inventory". This tool provided a screening of the applicants which was comprehensive. I understand that such instruments are commonly used now in various situations. The Foothills Hospital Training School, I think, followed the traditional pattern at first but its program became altered considerably. As you know, this school is still very active and one learns that the graduates are very much in demand. The older type of hospital nursing training has largely disappeared and the education of nurses has of course been taken over by the universities and colleges.

I enjoyed my association with the nursing education and the general ambience of the nursing school. We were called upon, in addition to teaching, to be included in their health care and to join with the nursing directors in any concern pertaining to students. Nursing educators now do not believe that the education of their students should involve another discipline such as medicine. I understand that they have divorced themselves from the earlier doctor-nurse relationship which was attributed to the example of Florence Nightingale.

Kirchner: Was any remuneration provided for any duties connected with the nursing schools?

McNeil: No! We considered any contribution a privilege or a responsibility to a colleague "to be".

Kirchner: You have said that you took part in the preceptorship type of program for young physicians at the General and Holy Cross Hospitals. Would you tell us something about this?

McNeil: There were no residency programs available in the city until after the presence of the medical school. The rotating internships offered by the two hospitals became very popular, giving as they did, a broad "hands on" experience for the young graduate physician. These young people are all graduates but are seeking further experience before entering general practice. The program still continues at the Holy, but it is not offered now at the General Hospital as they have their residency programs in the specialties and in general practice. The intern spent three months of the year each in Medicine, General Surgery, Gynecology and Obstetrics, and in Pediatrics. During this period he or she was associated with one or two members of the department but would have other responsibilities in the hospital, for example, Emergency. In addition to the ward experience some teaching or review lectures were made available. The interns were expected to take an active part in the preparation and presentation of ward rounds or other learning exercises. In medicine the intern worked up a new admission and give the orders for further diagnostic procedures or treatment. The intern was available to make rounds with you, or to be called upon for any matter dealing with patients. The review and discussion of cases, although always interesting, could take up long hours. I acted as a preceptor at both hospitals but as I became more deeply involved in Canadian Medical Association work and other things, the load was sometimes quite heavy. I am pleased to say that I was the preceptor for a number of the notable doctors practicing in the city now.

Kirchner: I believe you must have been a very busy man. Again, most teachers in the faculty, other than full-time people, receive an emolument although perhaps sometimes very small. Did you receive any monetary reward for this teaching work?

McNeil: No, there was no financial rewards, but as I have said there was considerable personal satisfaction. The preceptor benefited by the association and, "the teacher by the student will be taught."

EIGHTEEN

Kirchner: I would like you to tell us of the financial arrangements at the Calgary Associate Clinic, if you will.

McNeil: A salary was negotiated for the new arrival. When I returned with my Fellowship in Medicine, and following my years in the service, my salary was about $500.00 a month. I was now aged thirty-five, married, with one child. As a Flight Lieutenant in the Air Force I received about $300.00 per month. This money was taxable while one was in Canada.

Kirchner: Pretty nice.

McNeil: It did seem good at first, but as always it didn't go very far. I didn't own a home and I had to find some way to finance one. The bank would not be supportive in any manner; our families were not, at this stage, able to be helpful, and yet one way or another one had to establish a home, obtain insurance, start an R.S.P., etc. My home was built eventually, at minimum cost, by a contractor who by chance became very ill while we were dealing with him. This illness was an emergent acute process, and as a demonstration of gratitude upon his recovery, he offered to build our home at minimal building costs. The Clinic offered, beyond one's salary, an office with all supplies including a nurse, whose services were shared with two or three other doctors. Stenographic service was available and one stenographer did all the work of the office for some years. The dictaphones we used were at first the old fashioned reel types and we spoke into a hand held hornlike receiver. Before the reels could be used again they had to be shaved by the stenographer to erase the previous dictation. Most importantly, though, all of the accounting was done for us, and we were relieved of this tedium. It was our responsibility to advise the office of the cost of the services given.

Kirchner: Your salary, irrespective of how many patients you saw, did not change?

McNeil: The salary would be altered only once a year. The increments would be calculated by the executive, taking into consideration several factors. Only one of these factors was the amount one earned the previous year. If your income was less because of illness, involvement in community activities, or medical association work, your take-home pay would, within reason, not be reduced.

Later, following varying periods of association, an employee would be invited to join the partnership. This invitation was often delayed and the delay tended to produce unhappiness among the newer doctors. The delay was caused by financial obstacles: the older partners had placed much of their savings or estate into the institution. They naturally could not share this real property without compensation. The new doctors did not have the monies to lay out, the result of the time they had spent in the Service and in graduate study. They had become older, married, and their personal and family needs were urgent. Their desire to share in the direction and business control of their lives was being frustrated. These problems were eventually solved by separating the business ownership of the Clinic from the professional partnership. This was an improvement. However, one did sign an agreement before joining the group which, although probably necessary, was a source of some discomfort. This agreement prevented the doctor from leaving the Clinic and setting up a private practice in the vicinity of the city for a period of several years.

Kirchner: Was that a legal document?

McNeil: It was a legal document. The existence of this document was well known and was repugnant in the minds of other doctors who were not so restrained. If you did not develop a happy association with the group the only recourse was to leave the city. Having joined the partnership one could begin to build up a capital account; a portion of one's earnings being set aside to pay off the account of those doctors retiring. The new partner paid income tax on these monies which he would be unable to recover for a long time. The size of the capital account depended upon how much one could contribute; the high earners, such as the surgeons, had a distinct advantage. When I joined the partnership others with much less seniority than me had been partners for some time. The capital account system was abolished in 1965.

Kirchner: If I may ask, what happened with the accumulated capital account when the system was abolished?

McNeil: By this time the accounts had been reduced to manageable limits as the seniors had been largely paid off upon their retirement, etc. and the further settlement was not too difficult.

Kirchner: Surgeons must have received quite a lot?

McNeil: Yes, generally surgeons do have larger incomes, but I learned when I served on the executive for a period that this is not always so. One of our surgeons, a subspecialist, did not earn enough to provide for his own take-home pay, and therefore was (unknown to himself) subsidized by the rest of us. I found out, to my surprise, that in the year that I was President of The Alberta Medical Association my earnings from practice were so reduced, (the result of necessary absence), that I, too, was subsidized by my colleagues. This was something the group anticipated (perhaps not to such a great extent) when they gave their approval for me to assume these duties. Such was the attitude of Clinic doctors to their professional responsibilities. I wonder if a few moments might be spent on the illnesses and the fortunes that befell the original partners? In addition, perhaps I might have the opportunity to refer to doctors whom I may or may not have spoken of before?

Kirchner: It would be very interesting, yes.

McNeil: Dr. Macnab, who I have referred to often in an appreciative manner, led rather a stormy life, associated with constant tension. He gave such intensity to his work that he would be obliged to stop work from time to time. Dr. Scarlett would admit him to hospital where I recall that the diagnosis was that of the flu, but the extreme "sweats" he experienced I attributed to a psychomotor reaction associated with the letdown of work. He was not fortunate enough to have the support of a helpful wife; on the contrary, she regularly aggravated the situation by her strange behavior. I do not think that Dr. Macnab came to me first, but I well remember him standing in the door of my office and saying to me, "Mac . . . I can't see." I don't think that I would have examined him at that time, and I do not think it would have been appropriate for me to have done so, as Dr. Scarlett was his doctor. I suspect that he did not have a complete investigation either in Calgary or at the Mayo Clinic. An x-ray, however, did demonstrate an enlargement of the sella turcica, indicative of a pituitary tumor. He was treated at Mayo's and the tumor did respond at first to radiation with some recession of his symptoms. As he did not have obvious endocrine signs I would consider that the tumor was a Craniopharyngioma (these cells, of course, do not produce hormones). The disturbance of his vision represented the classical sign of pressure on the optic nerve fibers in the optic chiasma.

Kirchner: He was in his 70's then, wasn't he?

McNeil: I suppose that would be so. He was, however, very active up until the onset of these symptoms. A little later when, for a time, his care was my responsibility, I decided to send him to the Montreal Neurological Institute. Dr. Penfield had retired by that time but I had become well acquainted with the institute during my sojourn in Montreal. I had hoped that as Mayo's had not ventured to do a craniotomy or a surgical procedure to remove the tumor, that the Montreal Neurological Institute might. They, considering his age, probably wisely elected not to operate. Dr. Macnab deteriorated steadily and eventually concluded several more years as a vegetable . . . his worst fear! We did not have a neurosurgeon in Calgary for some years. Dr. Charles Taylor was our first, and prior to that, it was necessary to refer our problems elsewhere, sometimes to Dr. Hepburn or Dr. Guy Morton in Edmonton. Thinking of the latter doctor I recall referring him a lady with the Brown-Sequard Syndrome (as you know having signs of interference with the function of one half of the spinal cord). I further recall that I was accurate as to the site of the tumor within one dorsal cord segment.

Kirchner: Wasn't it Olivecrona in Stockholm who did successful pituitary tumor operations?

McNeil: Oh yes?

Kirchner: He was one of the men I believe who did that well in the early fifties.

McNeil: Dr. G. D. Stanley was well known to me. He was one of the early partners and a close friend to Drs. Macnab and Scarlett. Although a strict temperance man he was proud of his association with the famous Bob Edwards, in part a result of his first years in Alberta and his first practice in High River. Mr. Bob Edwards, although greatly revered, had problems with alcohol. I have mentioned Dr. Stanley's career as a Member of Parliament for Calgary, but he might be recognized for a number of other contributions, such as his personal support to Mount Royal College. You might have noticed the Dr. G. D. Stanley Gymnasium attached to the Kerby Centre (the original Mount Royal College). I had been called by him a number of times to administer a 10 cc. intramuscular injection of milk — a very satisfactory treatment for his recurrent Iritis. The milk would stimulate his immune system very satisfactorily and the inflamed eye would rapidly improve. Dr. Stanley suffered a typical coronary occlusion and I could not prevail upon him to enter hospital in time to accept suitable treatment. Mrs. Stanley, his beautiful and beloved wife had passed on, and I believe a sincere wish to carry on did not exist.

Kirchner: He died of that later?

McNeil: Yes. I was eventually able to take him to hospital but he lived only a few days, and he died from this massive occlusion. Dr. Scarlett lived out his life very fully, writing constantly and maintaining all of his interests almost to the end. It was in these latter years that I and others had the opportunity to spend rewarding hours with him. Dr. Fred Pilcher, the urologist, the southerner I have spoken of before, enjoyed a good reputation in the medical field and in the life of the community. Unfortunately, he was probably not truly known to most of us, and his career as an excellent surgeon and doctor ended when he committed suicide. Dr. Hugh Stuart, again a dedicated surgeon and doctor, was a highly sensitive man and many aspects of his personality were unknown to the majority of his colleagues. As alcohol was used more and more, and unfavorably influencing his home and work, he left Calgary taking up a practice in California. He, too, tragically ended his own life. Dr Alex Fisher, the obstetrician, whom I have said gave so much to his patients, was a wonderful family man. He died from complications of the "doctor's disease" (Scarlett's often stated axiom) a Coronary Occlusion. I became the physician to most of the old senior members such as Dr. Aikenhead and Mrs. Aikenhead. Dr. Aikenhead succumbed to cirrhosis of the liver, although remarkably he was a lifetime temperance adherent.

I look back very happily at my association with our colleagues in Edmonton and the University of Alberta's Faculty of Medicine. The offices of the Alberta College and the Alberta Medical Association while at first situated in Calgary, were properly moved later to Edmonton. I had occasion to be in Edmonton many times over the years. The associations with colleagues in other centres such as Lethbridge, Medicine Hat, Red Deer, etc. also evoke many pleasant memories. I cannot take time to acknowledge many of these but I would like to mention a few. Dr. John Scott stands out in my memory as he does so in the minds of so many of the physicians and others who knew him. Dr. Scott was referred to often, and quite deservedly, as "Mr. Medicine" and he was indeed a great doctor, teacher, and friend. It seemed that our welfare as a colleague was his personal responsibility. He would somehow find time to visit you or arrange that you visit with him and other doctors in Edmonton. He would somehow know that you were involved in a hassle on a hospital problem and would find a way of giving you support. When I addressed the Edmonton Academy of Medicine one evening, Dr. Scott was the first to open the discussion of my paper. During a quiet little talk with us he encouraged Dr. Thorson and I to join the American College of Physicians. This was valuable advice and the association with that body gave us the opportunity to attend the best medical sessions on this continent. The Royal College for various reasons could not at that time provide similar privileges. I have talked and written to him in regard to a worthy position that he championed. As you will know, Dr. Collip, the one time professor of biochemistry at Alberta, played a vital role in the discovery of insulin having, at least, as a member of the team, prepared the extract which made its use possible. Dr. McLeod under whose auspices, and in whose laboratory, the work was done shared his half of the Nobel prize in medicine with Dr. Collip. Dr. Banting acted similarly with Dr. Best. Dr. Collip, a very gentle man, did not challenge some men in Toronto who would attempt to stifle his part in the work. Dr. Scott resented this and I remember a visit I had with him on a plane one night; he was returning from Dr. Collip's humble funeral services in London. Dr. Best had passed away at about the same time and his obsequies had national recognition. I have some private correspondence from Dr. Scott, pertaining to the insulin story which I think should be more widely known. I have made mention of my friend Dr. Don Wilson who became Professor of Medicine, and who is still active.

A great deal of his attention is given to recording the history of medicine in Alberta. I think also of Dr. Irving Bell, another good friend of young physicians in Edmonton. Dr. Bramley Moore, the secretary of the Alberta College, was an example of propriety and dignity to all of us. I think of some of the fine doctors at Lethbridge, Dr. Hunt, Dr. Hague, and their associates, like my good friend Dr. Hugh Arnold, and Dr. Peter Campbell. In Red Deer, Drs. Parsons and associates, and in Medicine Hat, of Dr. MacCharles and the members of the Medicine Hat Clinic. These are only a very few of the fine men I have known in Alberta. During our first year of marriage Mary Lou became extremely ill. Living in MacLeod it eventuated that I took this very sick girl to hospital in Lethbridge. Because the illness was by that time diagnosed as mesles, Dr. Cairns, the pediatrician, took over the care of my unconscious wife. I well remember that he was to call in Dr. Peter Campbell (whom Lethbridge doctors considered the Dean of their medical community) for the wise advice they knew he could provide.

Kirchner: The Associate Clinic introduced several of the specialties to Calgary. Did this apply to cardiac surgery?

McNeil: Yes it did. When Dr. George Miller returned from his training at the Mayo Clinic in that specialty some effort had to be made to train surgical teams and to familiarize staff with the equipment to be used. This resulted in a venture which is worthy of chronicling. The Sisters at the Holy Cross made space available in an older building situated behind the present buildings. This was actually an earlier Holy Cross Hospital which had been abandoned as the hospital grew. Here they set up the heart pump and prepared to develop their skills with the use of dogs provided by the Calgary Animal Control people. They encountered some real difficulties when having to deal with the S.P.C.A. These things were overcome, obviously, and this paved the way for cardiac surgery in the city. It explains, too, the part the Holy Cross continues to play in that field. The Cardiac Surgeons have remained with the Clinic until the present time.

Kirchner: Was it Dr. Scarlett who might be considered the first cardiologist?

McNeil: General internists have frequently been referred to as cardiologists particularly by the layman. It is always difficult to describe the work of an internist. The layman can understand the work of a subspecialist such as a neurologist, or even a general surgeon. The designation of an internist as a cardiologist has often seemed to be a satisfactory description. As an internist, Dr. Willis Merritt would have preceded him.

NINETEEN

Kirchner: How was the socioeconomic situation in Calgary when you started to practice?

McNeil: When I first started way back in 1940, many people were on relief, the common term used for welfare, going back into depression times. The city looked in a rundown state, obviously the result of the austerity of the same depression. One could feel a sense of western welcome by the wonderfully friendly people of this community. I could recite many examples of this and I remember accepting an invitation to visit Banff. These awesome mountains had on me that strange unworldly feeling that many must feel, at least on the first visit. The highway to Banff was not paved entirely and has been improved a number of times before it reached its present condition. To be invited to spend a weekend at a ranch and to meet these very special people remains in my memory. Should you look out to the southwest any evening you would see the red sky; the result of the burning off of gas at Turner Valley. It was impressive to visit the oil field and the area called ''Hell's Half Acre'' where the gas was burned and wasted, as almost a useless by-product.

The people on relief could not pay anything for medical services or any other service. The city eventually offered doctors twenty dollars a month each as the total payment for all the relief patients under their care. This was somewhat of a boon as the doctors were able to influence the city to pay the same sum to the Calgary doctors who had enlisted and so for a period I was a recipient of this even while I was in Britain. Later, the Calgary Medical Society designated all the monthly allowances to their membership to be placed in a contingency fund to be used for doctors in the future who might be in financial difficulty. Some of this money still exists but much of it has been squandered in ways that the original fellows would not have approved. I remember that when I took over the presidency, Dr. Joe Follett met me at the Bank of Montreal so that I could verify the presence of the various bonds, etc. I attended to many very poor people particularly during my early years in Calgary. Mary Lou who, for a time, was a Victorian Order nurse, can attest to the presence of shabby ghettoes in the city; the Commercial building and the Beveridge building come to mind. The Milton Hotel was a bordello and the poorer class hotels

106

were centres for heroin and drug traffic. The Chinese kept to themselves, but their state was aggravated by the immigration laws preventing their wives from joining them. They tended to marry unfortunate white girls or lead a life of gambling and alcohol. To see the barren rooms of these oriental men was my doubtful fortune only too often. I recall treating one of the most wealthy of the gamblers in Chinatown for an infection process with a sulpha drug and to observe a remarkable phenomenon. The very peculiar irregular swelling in his hands, which had almost made his hands useless, changed while on the sulpha. The skin broke and a fluid exuded of a pussy nature, and in this fluid the characteristic "sulphur granules" of Actinomycosis were abundant. This was the first time I had ever seen these but their appearance was classical. The patient's problem had been written up previously and Dr. Scarlett had labelled the accompanying pictures as the "tophi" of gout in his submission to the Canadian Medical Journal. Venereal diseases in all its stages was common in Calgary. The late stages of syphilis had often originated in the previous war, when often the complete treatment was "one" injection of 606. The mayor of an Alberta city was one such example.

Kirchner: What could you do in Calgary socially, for distraction, at that time?

McNeil: Not very much as one thinks of it at first, but that is probably unfair when one thinks of it a little more. There were no fine restaurants as we know today. Those available catered to cattlemen and farmers as they came to the city to sell their cattle or to buy their supplies. One of the social events of the year, which still carries on its important function, was the annual Calgary Bull Sale. Farmers or cattlemen would come to town, treating it as a social event, whether they were interested in buying cattle or not. The other great event was the Calgary Stampede. The exhibition had something for all ages just as it has today. There was only one place which might be called gracious and that was the Palliser Hotel. One of the nicest things you could plan to do was to attend the supper dance in the hotel on a Saturday night. Here there was an orchestra, and along with a fine meal you could dance. You could reserve a table but as one was not supposed to have liquor this was kept under the table in a brown paper bag; you were expected to order the mix to go along with it.

Kirchner: But why couldn't you?

McNeil: Alcohol was sold by government liquor vendors and beer was available in the beer parlors situated in hotels. Dr. Scarlett told me of entertaining a Russian visitor and upon sitting down for a meal in the McDonald Hotel in Edmonton, the visitor placed a bottle of vodka on the table. When told why he must put this away immediately he said, "You call this freedom?" This is as far as prohibition of the twenties had relaxed up until that time. The beer parlors were segregated into rooms for the men, and rooms for the women, and there was no mixed drinking. Alcohol was not served in hotels or restaurants till some time after the war and then only in licensed premises; you still see signs "fully licensed" displayed at restaurants. It was much longer before liquor could be served on Sunday even with a meal. Bars are a relatively late development in Western Canada. Food, for a long time, was not permitted in a beer parlor.

There were parties among the modest number of fairly well to do people in this city. The oil business had been active for some time in the community and this was the source of some wealth. The major private clubs in the city were the Glencoe Club, the Renfrew Club, and the Ranchman's Club. The Glencoe Club was a family sports club and quite popular. We joined the club at a time when membership cost only two or three hundred dollars where now, if available at all and after a waiting period of a number of years, it is quite costly.

The Renfrew Club divided its membership and some of the members formed the Calgary Petroleum Club. The Ranchman's Club has not changed its chauvinist attitude towards women very much. Mixed gatherings are still held in a separate part of the building. One who was accustomed to having water sports and activites available would miss these in Southern Alberta where there are almost no warm lakes. It was necessary to develop an appreciation for the mountains and all the things they offered. I did some of my courting on that half day off on horseback riding with Mary Lou. There were very enthusiastic nimrods and the highways could be busy on the opening morning of duck shooting or upland bird season. The social life of the ranch and the farm was richer, I'm told. I cannot remember that there was any legitimate theater or a philharmonic orchestra.

Kirchner: Dr. McNeil, in that time did being a doctor in Calgary represent sort of a status symbol? For instance, these persons who became rich, did they consider it an honor if a physician accepted their invitation?

McNeil: Yes, I would feel that was so. We were treated in a rather respectful, dignified manner. There was no presumption to call you by your first name. I notice that my old patients still seem to feel uncomfortable to address me by anything other than Doctor. We received special consideration in a number of ways; we would be forgiven for our lateness, or leaving early, or our constant telephone interruptions at social gatherings. Our license plates would indicate our profession so that the policeman would permit us some laxity in our driving behaviour. I have often felt some degree of camaraderie with the police. We received special consideration in the courts so as to provide us with a convenient time for us to appear. The nurses enjoyed a higher status too, and the lack of such seems a topic in their labor negotiations now. The mutual respect of nurse and doctor was greater in my opinion then.

Kirchner: What about the movies?

McNeil: Yes, the movies were probably the most popular and regular social activity. A theater house like the "Capitol" was very ornate and would be packed with long waiting lines in its large lobbies or stretching out onto Eighth Avenue. One would likely dress well, as propriety expected, for such a night out.

Kirchner: This, I might say, would be an interesting thing to ask. Wives are always playing a leading role in social life: how do you see the wives of physicians of the time in this respect? Were they the initiators who brought people together, or would this rather come from the men, from the doctors?

McNeil: My first reaction was to say that the impetus to initiate social functions arose from the men. This is not right . . . I was reflecting upon the greater degree of male chauvinism attributed to times past. I was not happy with that response and as I ruminated upon your question, I decided to ask Mary Lou for her opinion. She rightly reminded me that then, the doctor's wife assumed a much more active role. It was the wife's responsibility to assist the new recently arrived doctor's wife in every way possible, so that her entry into the medical community would be with as much ease as possible. She might hold a reception of some type, be it a tea, and or a more elaborate event. She might host a smaller reception to provide introduction to the immediate colleagues of her husband or a larger party including a more comprehensive group. She, too, would assume responsiblity for a continuing role in social life. Mary Lou and I can think of social evenings in homes for dining or music where we might be expected to wear evening clothes. The social obligations apparently seemed to evoke some trepidation in a young matron. Once a year the Calgary Medical Society hosted "Calgary Ladies Night" and I believe this traditional event continues to take place. On that night we honored the ladies recognizing their contribution and sacrifices necessary to the achievements of their husbands. It is customary to offer a toast to the ladies and this was accomplished by selecting a good speaker who was expected to deliver a most charming address, acknowledging all of these things. The ladies would respond to this toast by asking the wife of the president to perform this function. In this regard I would like to tell you about one of these replies. For the year that I was the president of the society, Mary Lou was a patient at the Baker Sanatorium, recovering from the illness I would have told you about. When it was announced that Mrs. McNeil would now be asked to respond to the toast, the audience, as you can imagine, was perplexed. Her reply had been taped at the Sanatorim and when replayed on this occasion came out that evening loud and clear. I revelled of course in the compliments that came my way following her reply. My very good friend and colleague Dr. Alan Dixon had accomplished this, as he had done so many other times on behalf of Calgary doctors. This event was a formal party held at the Palliser Hotel.

TWENTY

Kirchner: Would you comment on how your average day went by in the fifties?

McNeil: I was prone to start my day a little slowly. Ward rounds, once or twice a week, (if I attended a General Hospital session) held usually at eight in the morning would force me to start earlier. At the hospital I would be joined by my intern and he would have picked up any notes which had collected since my last visit. These notes dealt with requests for consultation, etc. We would precede the patient visiting with a stop at the x-ray department and the laboratory so that we might review our day before responding to these requests. I found these stops most useful as it gave one time to assimilate the findings. I would have probably twenty patients under my name but these might, for example, be patients admitted under others, or pre and post surgical cases which might have required my attention at some point. The rounds might necessitate a visit to every ward in the hospital including pediatrics and obstetrics. On those latter wards the problems might be those of diabetes or blood disease, etc. Many interruptions to your progress around the hospital would occur when you were called to the telephone or required to speak with concerned families. These latter stops you could expect, but one had to have forbearance to deal with the frequent interruptions sometimes called the "curbstone consultation". These accostments were informal, and occurred when a doctor has some indecision or concern over a problem, but had not yet decided to request a formal consultation. Such stops made it difficult indeed to plan one's day and took a great deal of time. The unexpected, often emergent situations, would occur. Requests to see a nurse or a sister late in the morning after other interruptions could increase my concern about getting through the morning. Hospital committee meetings had to be planned for, but for some of these such as hospital executive meetings, lunch might be included. The attendance at a Cancer Clinic session would take an entire morning, and for that day the hospital work was done by the intern or by myself in the evening. Nurses' lectures would require an hour or two for several days in the year but this work was shared among several doctors. On the weekends, the internists eventually worked out an on call roster which permitted breaks and time off but the work was heavy for the internist on call. I think I have said before

111

that intensive care facilities developed only later; for the first years they had no full-time medical staff. The internists were responsible for most of the patients admitted to those facilities.

Kirchner: Did you have time to stop for a cup of coffee?

McNeil: Oh yes, and perhaps I have over-emphasized how hard I worked. Much of my problem was of my own making — my tardiness and failure to plan my day well. They were busy times though and when I think back to some periods, such as our polio epidemics, one can wonder how I did get through it all. Yes, we would stop regularly by the operating room for coffee, a smoke, and often a necessary visit with a surgeon about mutual patients . . or most importantly to discuss the recent Stampeder game.

Kirchner: And then you started again?

McNeil: Yes. I usually had a few (perhaps three or four) patients at the General Hospital and as I have said, I had preceptor responsibilities there. There may have been other General Hospital duties such as committee meetings. Perhaps I will have time to tell you about one or two of the more interesting developments that I was associated with at that hospital.

Kirchner: How did you do this? You were shuttling between the two hospitals?

McNeil: I wonder now too, how I spread myself so thin. I did not visit the General nearly as often as the Holy Cross. One used weekends and slack days to catch up and do such jobs as completion of records.

Kirchner: This could mean a nonstop day from 9 o'clock with a coffee break at two?

McNeil: Unless I had a luncheon meeting, the meal would be a quick snack at a hospital cafeteria and this custom remains so now with most doctors. I would regularly arrive at my office late. The nurse would have additional patients to those already arranged by appointment. She would also have a report for me which would probably include some urgent telephone calls. The patients seen would include those referred from other physicians in or outside of our own office. Many, however, would be properly classified as private patients. The role of a personal physician who might be a specialist was common then, but has largely disappeared in Canada now since the onset of universal medicare. The place of a doctor and a specialist as a personal physician still flourishes in the United States. There the patient can expect that his heart disease or diabetes will receive the continuing care of a doctor having specialized training. Perhaps the explanations for this, as I see it, could be discussed at another time. It would not be uncommon for me to be called out to some other city such as Drumheller or High River to see a patient in consultation.

Kirchner: And then you'd go?

McNeil: This often was very pleasant, particularly if I was required to remain overnight. Mary Lou would sometimes go along with me if she could make suitable arrangements for the children. It could be most pleasant; the doctor requesting the consultation might arrange a little reception following the patient visit and this would include other doctors and their wives. It might be interesting for you to know that the charges submitted would amount to, I believe, 50 cents a mile. I was called to see a lady in High River one night and made a diagnosis of a subdural hematoma. She was unconscious and I recommended that she be transferred to Calgary. Following craniotomy, she recovered, but as she had never seen me until she was conscious, she refused to accept my charges, while fully acknowledging those of the neurosurgeon.

Returning to my day, I would not finish at the office until 7:00, either before or after supper. It was difficult to get through the many phone calls which would collect during the day. When I mention that a certain number of house calls were made during the week it seems that I am exaggerating the amount of work which I did.

Perhaps I could be forgiven for the proclivity that I enjoyed, the anticipation of a drink before the evening meal. I think of a very nice custom that one or two of my patients observed (they may have been Scotch or European) and that was to insist that the doctor sit down, (the call being at the end of a day) for a glass of scotch before he embraced the medical problem at hand.

Kirchner: This amount of work must have put you under an enormous stress.

McNeil: Yes, but while I have detailed my work schedule emphasizing the quantity of work, I have not said much about the satisfaction that I received from it. We enjoyed an enviable position in the community in the perception of many people. We were called upon as resource people to counsel and address various groups. When we accompanied the diabetic society at their annual camp for diabetic children, we were encouraged to bring our own families along. Our children would join the diabetic youngsters, take part in their programs, and share as much of a holiday as the diabetic campers. Such an experience, I'm sure, was an excellent one for our children as they saw the insulin injection, the diabetic reactions, and various problems of their roommates. I did become fatigued and, as you know, one becomes slow and less efficient then. These effects were felt by our families, but I believe they were able to appreciate the situation. One of the benefits I recognized, after relinquishing the cigarette habit, was the decrease in fatigue and the increase of efficiency.

TWENTY ONE

Kirchner: Among the books we received from the Clinic Library we found an enormous quantity of journal clippings from the Calgary Herald dealing with the progress of the National Health Care Plan. Do you have any explanation? Why it is that all this information has been collected about the Health Care Plan? Did they oppose this at the Clinic at that time?

McNeil: No, most doctors were not opposed to health insurance. It was realized that some form of national or government intervention or "state medicine" was inevitable. To avoid a monolithic system and the bureaucratic supervision of the profession which would evolve, the medical profession developed their "doctor-sponsored" medical insurance schemes in every province of Canada. National Health Care, as it existed then and still does in places such as Britain, was reprehensible to doctors. Most English people have known nothing else and although may have little regard for their "panel" doctor they accept the system . . . but not entirely. As you probably know many people in England seek, if they can possibly afford it, private medical care outside the state system. These private services are sponsored in large part, I understand, by American business interests. The doctors in Alberta developed the Medical Services of Alberta Incorporated (M.S.I.). This was supported by almost all physicians but, of course, a few would not trust this plan either. For those doctors who supported the scheme, they agreed to accept, at first, as full payment, a little over eighty percent of the scheduled fee. The premiums were paid by the individual, or in full or in part by the employer. As time passed there was increasing acceptance of the plan by the public, industry, and the medical profession. The provincial doctor-sponsored schemes had advanced to the point where they could provide portability of benefits from one province to another. The system was working well in every province and was economically viable, supporting itself without government subsidy. When the federal government implemented its plan it was necessary to make all other plans illegal. We were obliged to close the M.S.I. Alberta operation, cancelling all of the contracts. The politicians such as Tommy Douglas, who were prime movers of the federal plan, could not rest until medical care became a government benefit entirely. The attitude of Mr. Douglas had always been difficult for me to understand. As a young person, Mr. Douglas required a great deal of medical care which I presume must have been successful, and very important to his life. Possibly as a minister he resented the fact that doctors would not accept fees from the clergy. It is quite unfair, in my opinion, to state that the political plan was better than that of the doctor-sponsored plans. The doctor-sponsored plans could have been supported so that they could offer universal coverage. Certain funds remained in the coffers of M.S.I. (Alberta) and this has grown greatly over the years. I think we can be quite proud of the research projects which they have supported. The whole pattern of practice changed after the application of the government scheme. Many doctors, I might say, have tended to "work to rule" since. They have objected to many of those things that we accepted as our responsibility and the new young men may look upon our behavior as foolish and gratuitous. Some general practitioners now have given up night and domicilary work. Many seem to have forsaken the Hippocratic admonition that "the responsibilities of their calling must come before all else". These same doctors take an entirely opposite stand: that the practice of medicine must not interfere with their private life. The doctor's wife, too, does not see her position as one of sacrifice to support the ideals of this profession and the work of her husband. The family enjoys the rewards, and he demands that he receive full recompense for each and every service he provides. I doubt that their homes are more stable or that their children are more successful than ours. The busy doctor/father, always concerned with the welfare of others, represented an example which many children tried to emulate or at least was a source of some pride to them. I realize that many doctors practicing today were raised in a medical household. The responsibilities to the patient now are minimal, and often limited to that one visit. Doctors restrict the number of people in their practice and the number of patients they will see in the day. They close the office in the late afternoon having no further responsibility until the next day. They may not follow their patient in the hospital or plan to follow the course of the illness at home. They may indeed limit their work to office practice, considering that hospital or home care is not "time management" profitable. Their large incomes are assured if they properly provide the computer with the information required. The work, of course, must be done by someone and so it is often left to the specialist, the social worker, or paramedic people. I believe many doctors lead a rather dull life unable to know the enjoyment or satisfaction which may come with a fuller career. Increasing numbers of people are employed in the medical care field and costs rise to astronomical proportions. The relationship between nurses and doctors has all changed and nurses realize that their independent role is of increasing importance. They rightly believe that they do not receive sufficient recognition or recompense for their contribution. Their respect for, and the amount of cooperation which they are inclined to offer to physicians, continues to diminish. Philanthropy has been taken away from medical services and economy in its provision is not practiced. Monies are spent by the socially conscious person to assist one "unfortunate" individual for travel and service to some distant place, rather than contributing to a project, which might help many. The patient accepts minimal responsibility. He is not required to even be gracious and may visit as many doctors as he likes at no expense to himself. The doctor abuses the system by doing too much lab work, x-ray examination, consultation, etc. At the hospital, the family is in no hurry to return the patient home, particularly if they are "old" or if he cannot be conveniently cared for. The hospital beds are so fully occupied by chronic problems that there is no room for the younger, more urgent problems. The hospitals have very costly administrative staffs. Government sponsored medical care has had great benefits, but it has altered this ethos and not always for the best.

Kirchner: I heard that in the U.S. many people without health insurance accumulated a debt for as much as $40,000 to $80,000 because of illness. There are cases when the family's possessions were wiped out because they couldn't pay the doctor's bill. So I believe this is the other extreme.

McNeil: It is unfortunate that the indiviual on one side, in the United States, carries so much liability. The cost of medical services is not too different here than in the United States. The U.S. citizen who takes ill in Canada will be charged for services here, not much less than he would be at his home. Canada cannot provide services really much cheaper than their neighbors. The individual American shoulders too great a burden for his medical care and it is possible that people are denied or forego necessary services because of economic considerations. There are benefits in the U.S. system though. For example, the availability of hospital beds and the privilege to select your own doctor, be he a specialist or a G.P. A Canadian is always obliged to enter the system through a G.P. and as an "outdoor" hospital patient he does not have freedom to select his doctor. I support the stand that the patient in Canada should be aware of the cost of a service and if able, should bear a portion of the expense. This has been the position taken by our colleagues of the Canadian Medical Association . . . an attitude unacceptable I know to politicians . . . but not all thinking people.

Kirchner: Exactly; there must be middle ground.

TWENTY TWO

Kirchner: I would like you to tell us something about the Calgary Medical Society.

McNeil: The Calgary Medical Society has been rather important to doctors in Calgary.

Kirchner: When you arrived in the city was the Society flourishing?

McNeil: Yes, it was. It has been in existence for a long time. I began to attend meetings soon after my arrival. I have already mentioned one event, the Annual Ladies Night. Business or scientific meetings would be held once a month in the winter time. As for the scientific sessions I remember being impressed (having come from a teaching center) that the speakers were commonly local doctors, with virtually no qualification on the subject, but who had made a good effort to "bone-up" on the subject for the evening. This changed of course with time. It was common ground where doctors could come together outside their office or hospital. It was following my return to Calgary with my specialty that I became involved more closely with the Society. I was invited first to look after speakers for the meetings of the Society and I made some effort to bring in guest speakers. I was not provided with money for this nor was there any money available. I had some success in attracting speakers who would come "gratis" such as one who might be able to stop off while making a trip for some other reason. If the speaker was travelling to Edmonton to give an address, he/she could be asked if he would stop by Calgary for the same purpose. I remember that one of those speakers was Dr. P. H. T. Thorlakson, who I have mentioned before in reference to the department of surgery at the University of Manitoba. He was the motivator and the creator of the large Winnipeg Clinic and later of its offshoot, The Winnipeg Foundation. The executive of the Calgary Medical Society met frequently and assumed responsibilities to the profession of the city, for the welfare of doctors, for the handling of complaints or criticisms of patients, and for the relationships of the profession to the media. Its goals, as I see them, are that of relating the profession to the community and upholding the principles of our calling. Having had some success with education programs, I continued to be active and eventually became the president of the Society. My year as the president went along very well and I don't remember that there were any remarkable occurrences over the period, and I made many friends.

Kirchner: Other than what you have told us, did the Calgary Medical Society have any official status at that time?

McNeil: No. The Calgary Medical Society was and is a voluntary organization. It might be considered as a small unit or a grass root of the Canadian Medical Association. It is not incorporated, and has no power over the profession, such as discipline. The Alberta and the Canadian Medical Associations are voluntary too, and possess no legislated power over the profession. The Associations act for the profession in negotiations with government, and through its various committees and councils, establish the doctors' position on health matters which is of broad interest to the public. Doctors, and there are many, who are not members, enjoy the benefits of these negotiations and the attention which members give to the problems of the day. The legal body which directs the profession under the Medical Professions Act is the College of Physicians and Surgeons of Alberta. It has full powers to grant or remove licenses, to discipline, and to fine its members. The College membership is compulsory and its authority is delegated by the government through the Medical Professions Act. The College has been guided for a long time with great wisdom by its Registrar, my long-standing and good friend Dr. L. H. Le Riche, whom I'm sure you will have seen frequently quoted by the press and other media.

Kirchner: How many members were there at that time in the Calgary Medical Society?

McNeil: In 1940, there were perhaps 75 doctors in the city, but of course not all of them joined the Society. The percentage of membership of those practicing then might have been greater than it is now. With the advent of the medical school, the Calgary Medical Society became less important and the new teaching physicians have shown a varying interest in its activities. There are, of course, a good number of the university faculty who believe the Society should be supported and take part in its activities.

Kirchner: What is your recollection of the University of Calgary?

McNeil: In 1960, the University of Calgary consisted of only two buildings, the Arts and Education building, and the Science building. When I first recall visiting the university the buildings were new and surrounded by bare land without grass, trees, or shrubbery. The dust in those first summers was everywhere. I think that the next building which evolved was the Physical Education structure. The university, as you probably know, had grown out of the old Normal School or teachers college, which was part of the Southern Alberta Technical Institute. The teacher college background explains the title "Principal" which Dr. Malcom Taylor was called when he was in Calgary. He succeeded Dr. Doucette in this position. The university was at first only a branch of the University of Alberta at Edmonton. As I understand it, Edmonton originally received the provincial university in a trade off with Calgary, which received the Superior Courts and their facilities in lieu of this. It was first suggested that the two universities be called the University of Alberta at Edmonton and University of Alberta at Calgary. This did not satisfy those strong advocates of automony for the University at Calgary. Dr. Taylor had been employed in some capacity by the Canadian Medical Association at a previous time. Through this association he had become acquainted with Dr. Harry Morgan of our office, who as I have said was very active in Association work. Dr. Taylor contacted Dr. Morgan and apparently asked that he recommend a doctor who might assume responsibility for the medical care of students. Dr. Morgan passed this along to me. "I don't know what is required for Student Health Services, but you look into it will

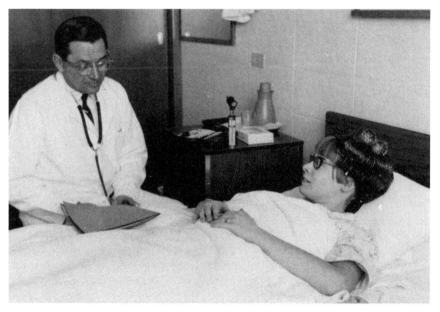

University of Calgary, Student Health Services, ca 1970.

you?'', he said. My involvement with the university commenced then.

The health service consisted of two small rooms set aside in the Arts building. The reception area was shared with the head of the department of Classics. An excellent nurse was the only staff with the exception of a part-time stenographer. I visited the Principal to learn what might be expected. I remember that he expressed his concerns as to the medical attention, if any, that students might be receiving. I think he expressed some concern as to a hazard of suicide amongst these young people. I naively evaluated the situation and agreed to visit the health service for an hour possibly twice a week.

Kirchner: Excuse me, did he tell you of any suicide epidemics among the students at that time?

McNeil: Yes, but I did not realize that the subject was receiving so much attention at universities at the time. Dr. Armstrong, the succeeding president, from some previous experience had very definite concerns in this regard. I contacted the director of Student Health at Edmonton. This was Dr. Frank Elliott, an internist who was well known to me. He was also the close associate of Dr. John Scott, the head of the department of medicine whom I have spoken of before. Dr. Scott carried on a large full-time practice of medicine while also carrying out his university duties. Apparently he had directed his partner to attend to the Student Health Service. This Dr. Elliott did for many years while he, too, carried on his own busy practice. I imagine that I assumed that if Frank could carry on a practice and look after student health I could do the same. Dr. Elliott directed the health service for many years as a personal contribution to the university and accepted no reimbursement for the work. I was not quite so magnanimous. During a telephone conversation with the bursar at Edmonton I agreed to take on the work for the generous reward of seven hundred and fifty dollars a year. These monies were, of course, directed to the business office at the Clinic. This arrangement was approved by Dr. Scarlett and Dr. Morgan. The university was growing rapidly and the demand upon me increased similarly. Dr. Taylor called upon me regularly with regard to faculty and staff. The faculty called upon me for any health matter and the requirements of students became greater. I realized then that I must have more doctors to carry out the work.

Kirchner: Where did you receive the patients?

McNeil: At the Health Service office in the university. To increase the doctor services I obtained the support, I think, of all the internists in town. This provided a doctor for a short time each day and these specialists did the work for something like fifteen dollars a visit. The obvious need for a psychiatrist was met by appealing to the Calgary Psychiatric Society. They arranged for one of their members to be available for clinics once or twice a week alternating the designated doctor each year. As the demand for services increased the internist arrangement was not adequate and other doctors were employed on a full day basis.

Kirchner: And who paid for this?

McNeil: The University paid for this. The students would indirectly pay through their fees, but as you know the fees contribute only a small part to the cost of the operation of a university. We started a pharmacy when I realized that students were often unable to pay for the prescribed medication. I saw a student who developed rheumatic heart disease because he was not able to pay for the penicillin ordered for him the year before.

Kirchner: Because he didn't have enough money?

McNeil: Yes, he didn't have the money. I employed a pharmacist too, after a young man (the pharmacist at a nearby drug store) came in one day, looking for some opportunity to utilize his time more fully. The presence of a pharmacist provided the professional and legal requirements for the handling of drugs.

McNeil: Dr. Herbert Armstrong, the first "president" of the University of Calgary, and I became good friends and were mutually supportive. As an example of his support, he recommended that I should have the opportunity to have a variety of exposures to universities all over Canada and the United States. In these "halcyon" days of Alberta I was given the opportunity to take a nurse (Miss Patricia Huff), another doctor (Dr. Don Wallace) and two of the business administrators on a great trip. We visited many universities, including those in Boston, New York, and as far as Miami as well as those in Canada. Dr. Armstrong showed his support for health services in many ways. I enjoyed freedom to direct the service as I saw fit. I was able to employ physicians new to the city, this being of mutual help to the doctor and the health service. A number of the busy physicians practicing now were helped at first by employment at the Student Health Service. In this regard I might mention Dr. Jim Clapperton, Dr. Peter Dunham, and several of their associates. A sports physician and a number of specialist consultants were available on a regular basis. Again, Dr. Armstrong insisted that the university have an infirmary without delay. To this end, space and staff were provided to operate a twenty-four hour "in patient" facility. The health service approached a degree of excellence, and maintained the respect of its student patients, the Calgary doctors, and the community in general. I somehow carried on my own work which was immensely satisfying, but difficult, while trying to do all the jobs I had become involved in. One activity I enjoyed was that of a cancer clinic consultant and there I was required to be present for at least one half day a week. Again it might be of interest to mention that the remuneration for this was $35.00 for the morning's work. I realized that I did not have time to carry on with the health service in addition to all of these other things I was doing, and so I made efforts to find a replacement. I brought in a man to take it over but this did not turn out very well. I tried to find others to take on the work such as the very fine internist Dr. Henry Shewchuk, who became ill and so had to make other plans. I suppose it was not necessarily my responsibility to find a replacement, but I was reluctant to abandon the work I had started.

TWENTY THREE

Kirchner: What about the Alberta Medical Association?

McNeil: I had been a representative for the Calgary district to the Board of Directors of the Alberta Medical Association for a period commencing in the late fifties. This required attendance at meetings in Edmonton several times a year. The association was then called the Alberta Branch of The Canadian Medical Association. The work of the Association deserves some explanation. The Alberta Medical Association employs a full-time Secretariat. The activity of the association is planned through the reports of various committees and their recommendations are directed through the Board of Directors to the annual meeting of the Association. A description of these committees might help to alter the opinion of some, that the medical associations are self-interest groups concerned only with the welfare of their members. The committees are, namely: Aging, Alcohol and Drug Abuse, Archives, Operative Deaths, Cancer, Child Health, Communications, Ethics, Hospitals, Membership Benefits such as group insurance, Pharmacy, Public Health, Rehabilitation, Maternal Mortality, and Reproductive Care. The Associations are not wealthy, either, as they are sometimes alleged to be. The national body, The Canadian Medical Association, is financed in the larger part by advertising in its journal. It is perhaps more affluent now, in that an offshoot of the Association manages certain investment funds belonging to its members. I became the chairman of an important national committee, the Pharmaceutical Committee. I gave a great deal of time to this and I think I enjoyed a measure of success in the work. This was in the time frame of the great disaster resulting from the introduction of Thalidomide. The duties of this committee required me to be a member of the Advisory Committee to the Food and Drug Division of The Department of Health, and I attended its meetings from time to time in Ottawa. It was at that time that the labelling of drugs with the provision of warnings as to potential side effects became compulsory.

My work with the pharmacy committee was followed by another even more time consuming endeavor, namely the presidency of the Alberta Medical Association. I did not seek the position and neither Mary Lou or myself wanted the job. We were prevailed upon by others

DOCTORS MEET
Officials of the Canadian Medical Association. Dr. D. L. McNeil, Alberta, President; Dr. R. O. Jones, Halifax, National President; Dr. A. D. Kelly, Toronto, National General Secretary; Dr. H. W. Horner, Barrhead, Alberta; Dr. R. K. Thomson, Edmonton, National President Elect.

including the Associate Clinic to take on the position. This was a memorable year for us. As president-elect I had the privilege to travel the length and breadth of this wonderful province for the purpose of visiting and making myself known to the profession. We travelled as a group with the secretary, Dr. Bob Woolstencroft, a scientific speaker Dr. John Dawson, a representative of the medical faculty at Edmonton, a Dr. Sam Kling, who spoke of new plans of the medical school for "Continuing Medical Education". My contribution was a (boringly long) paper on the Sociology of Medicine. As an officer of the Alberta Medical Association I became a representative on the General Council of the Canadian Medical Association. At the annual meeting held in Halifax I raised the subject of the hazards of suicide to the university student. I did not expect the national response I evoked. The press, I remember, seated in their area, through a rather humdrum afternoon, immediately sprang to attention when I spoke. Dr. Wodehouse of the University of Toronto (the dean of Canadian Student Health Services), and myself became the centre of media attention, as evidenced by the headlines in papers across the country. Examples of this tragic event had occurred in Halifax recently and the subject was indeed topical. I represented the Association on the Council of the College of

Physicians and Surgeons, and learned more of the subjects they would deal with, such as discipline, etc. It was an eventful year, too, in that we had at least one major confrontation with government, and this brought about an emergency meeting of all Alberta doctors held in Red Deer. My good friend and the dedicated Minister of Health, Dr. Donovan Ross was forced to back off his proposed legislation bringing the government into the control of "out patient" services.

Kirchner: What is your recollection of the development of the Medical School in Calgary?

McNeil: I have perused the minutes of the Board of Directors of the Alberta Medical Association, searching for references pertaining to the medical school at the University of Calgary. I find that my predecessor, as President of the Alberta Association, Dr. Hugh Arnold, at a meeting with the Board of Directors in 1963, raised the subject first. The board was asked, "Should we be making some effort to consider the development of a medical school in Calgary?" In 1964, while I was president of the Alberta Medical Association, the minutes indicate that following my raising this subject again, the Board created a committee to deal with this subject. The Committee was directed to arrange an appointment with Dr. H. Armstrong, of the University of Calgary, to discuss the subject. The committee members were, as I recall, Dr. H. E. Duggan, Dr. G. S. Balfour of the University of Lethbridge (which at the time was still affiliated with the University of Alberta), Dr. John Morgan, Dr. John Dawson (the chairman of the Education Committee of the Alberta Medical Association) and myself as the chairman.

Before arranging the meeting with the university president, we made, I think, a wise decision, and this was to visit Dr. Scarlett. He was, by this time, the Chancellor Emeritus of the University of Alberta, and we were certain that he could give us sound advice with regard to our actions. The committee presented our plans sitting down with Dr. Scarlett in his library at home. His advice was clear, and as we expected, very worthwhile: "Before and indeed after you meet with the president do not do anything in a coercive manner, do not make any announcement to the media in this regard — leave it to the president." I do not know the exact date that we saw Dr. Armstrong, but it was the fall of 1964 when he greeted us in the Arts building. It seemed to me that he was expecting our request and his response was positive from the outset. We learned that he did have some very definite opinions about such a faculty, and these had been developed in part through associations and discourse with other university administrators. Some of his tenets were not upheld later, such as the geographic location and the university control of the hospital.

Kirchner: There is one thing which is surprising. The population of Alberta was less than two million people, yet much larger cities, for instance, Vancouver, may have needed another medical school. Why it is, then, that it was Alberta who decided to have another medical school?

McNeil: I think that your question is most reasonable. The Province of British Columbia had been very slow (one might say derelict in their responsibility) in the development of their present faculty. On the other hand, Saskatchewan had for years before B.C. provided the two pre-medical, and the first two years of the medical course. The faculty at Manitoba had been in operation for more than a half century and the University of Alberta for a somewhat shorter time. The Royal Commission on Health Services had made a recommendation that a medical faculty should be developed in Calgary, and in priority, only second to one developed in Hamilton. The Social Credit government, in the now prosperous Alberta, may well have thought that acting upon this socially responsible recommendation it would not only be feasible financially but politically valuable. The government was generous to the electorate and people during these times. I think that later governments may have wondered too as to the wisdom of this decision. Dr. Armstrong promised us that our proposition would receive his careful thought and attention. He told us then that before he made any such recommendation to the Senate and the Board of Governors of the university, he would seek and be guided by counsel of medical educators both in Canada and beyond. He advised us that he would, if at all possible, insist upon certain other conditions. He believed that the teaching hospital, while not in itself needing to be large, must be geographically situated on the main campus and be under the administrative control of the university. He quoted another president, "If you develop a medical school, never make the mistake of not having your hospital right on campus. It must be an integral part of the university." As you know, this didn't happen.

The Foothills Hospital was already in place as a Provincial Government Hospital. Dr. Armstrong didn't believe that the university hospital should be a great ten storey edifice. His thinking was that it should consist of a small hospital providing the basic training in medicine, general surgery, obstetrics and pediatrics. The President advised us shortly of his "modus operandi" for the study of this proposal of ours. He had made arrangements to bring to Calgary a panel of three outstanding medical educators and this "triumvirate" would agree to meet interested parties here. These groups who would meet the triumvirate would consist of representatives from government, the present faculty of the University of Calgary, the Faculty of Medicine at Edmonton, and the medical profession of the city and of Alberta. He would make his recommendations to the Senate and the Board of Governors based upon their report. He provided us with the names of the triumvirate. These were to be Sir Charles Illingsworth Kerr, professor of neurological surgery at the University of Glasgow, Dr. J. A. MacFarlane, former dean of the Toronto Medical School, and Dr. George Wolff, Vice President for Medicine at the University of Virginia.

Dr. Armstrong asked me to arrange for the part of the hearing which would involve the medical profession. The selection of myself was natural I think, for, as a chairman of the Alberta Medical Committee, and President of the Association, I was also well known to him through his Student Health Service. I believe that I chose a broad representation of the profession and on the day that we met with these three noted men we had a representation of some fifty people. I may well have forgotten some but I will try to list the doctors and indicate my reasons for their choice. From Edmonton and the Faculty of Medicine were Dr. H. E. Duggan (radiology), Dr. O. Rostrup (orthopedics), Dr. Y. Yoneda, Dr. E. Haines, Dr. Sam King (surgeon), Dr. Lloyd Grisdale (President of the College of Physicians and Surgeons), Dr. Robert Woolstencroft (Secretary of the Alberta Medical Association). From Lethbridge, Dr. Hugh Arnold, Dr. Sig. Balfour, and from Drumheller, Dr. Roy LeRiche. I cannot recollect that anyone was present from Medicine Hat, but I must have invited some representative such as Dr. Don Lewis, an internist, and I think a member of the Board then. From Calgary, Dr. John Duffin (pathology), Drs. Irial Gogan and Dr. Cob. Johnson (hospital administrators), Dr. J. S. Gardner (veterans affairs and the Belcher hospital), Dr. Bob Pow (surgeon), Dr. John Crichton (pediatrician), Dr. Hugh Gallie (surgeon), Dr. John Morgan (cardiologist), Dr. Morris Carnat (psychiatrist), Dr. Maurice Vernon (President of the Calgary Medical Society), Dr. Harry Brodie (gynecology and later to become the first professor), Dr. Bob Wintemute (gynecologist), Dr. J. Hemstock (anesthesia), Dr. John McAllister (obstetrics), Dr. Howard McEwen (internist), Dr. Steve Thorson (internist and a member of the Board of Governors of the University), and Dr. Joe Moriarty (general practice). I believe that I had consulted the various societies such as the Psychiatric Society, etc. to name their selections.

Representatives of the nursing profession were present and I know that in the earliest plans the school was to be integrated with that profession.

We met with this august group in a large room of the Arts building and spent several hours with them. The three men sat at a large table in front of us and proceeded to field questions from all of us. The most vocal of the three doctors was Dr. MacFarlane and I recall some of his questions in particular. ''Do you really want this? Do you realize the work involved? Would you be ready to give your time? Would you teach? If you truly want this, it is not enough to say that you'll support it. You'll have to give all you have to make this thing go.'' Later in

126

the day he confessed that he was tremendously impressed by the degree of support that we had shown. He told us, too, of the similar impressions that the triumvirate was receiving from other than the profession. The triumvirate, of course, met with other faculty heads and members to learn for themselves the attitude these people would have to the presence of this new department. I understand that the other departments were supportive with the caveat that the school would not be isolated, but rather become closely associated with the rest of the institution. I think they envisioned exchanges of teaching resources and facilities. I do not think that this ever eventuated and it was a source of disappointment to them. The medical faculty at Edmonton was supportive as they did not believe that they should attempt to enlarge their enrollment. The triumvirate moved on to Edmonton where they met with Premier Manning and the cabinet and with the Chief Justice of Alberta, Mr. Justice Cairns. I might say that Mr. Cairns was very favorably inclined towards the University of Calgary, and he and his wife were patients of Dr. Thorson and sometimes myself. Dr. Thorson played a rather key role in this story and this should rightfully be told by him. Steve Thorson had been named to the Senate of U of C and the senate named him as their representative to the Board of Governors of U of C. The chairman of the board, Mr. Thorseen, was opposed to the development of the medical school at Calgary. This might have quashed the whole project if Dr. Thorson had not acted as he did. I cannot remember the details of the process, but Dr. Thorson made a motion upon some subject for which it was impossible for Mr. Thorseen to oppose. In some manner this resulted in the resignation of the chairman, and the later full support for the medical school by the Board of Governors.

The visit of the three distinguished doctors was concluded by a reception for them and their wives and members of the university which included Mary Lou and myself. I am reminded of the charming Mrs. Wolff, who was a writer of some note, and my companion at dinner. One of her books was entitled, *Anything Can Happen in Vermont*.

Kirchner: The "triumvirate" reported to whom?

McNeil: To Dr. Armstrong. I expect that you are familiar with the report. I obtained a copy from the Archives Department of the University recently. I have been trying of late to put some of the story together for the College of Physicians and Surgeons of Alberta, who are making an effort to update the history of medicine in Alberta. The conclusions of the report I have written down are as follows: "We believe there is a need to begin planning now for a new medical school in the Province of Alberta. The most suitable site for such a school is the City of Calgary. The province has just been able to keep up with its supply of doctors by virtue of immigration from other countries. The flow of immigration can easily change. Moreover, it is highly desirable that as many young Canadians as are qualified to enter medicine and have the desire to devote their lives to some of the branches of modern medicine, should be able to pursue the necessary studies against the very urgent needs for more doctors, both in our own country and in other rapidly developing areas of the world.'' The report of the commission, and its recommendations was signed by its three members. The recommendations are as follows:

1. Within the next 12 months the University should seek a suitably qualified dean who would be entrusted with the further planning for a medical school in Calgary.

2. The school should be an active and integral faculty of the University of Calgary.

3. In planning for future needs, provision should be made for the setting up in due time of a School of Dentistry and a School of Nursing, as well as for the provision of training in the ever increasing number of paramedical and allied professions.

4. The planning should include a University owned and operated hospital of not less than 350 beds, with provision for a further 50 to 100 beds if this is justified by the total need for hospital beds in the City of Calgary at the time that it is being built.

5. The plans included closed teaching units in all the active general hospitals in Calgary, notably in the Calgary General Hospital, the Holy Cross Hospital, and the Foothills General Hospital.

''It is noted that even if the initial plans are undertaken within the next 12 months, we do not see the possibility of a first class graduating before 1975.''

TWENTY FOUR

I would like to quote further from the commission's report so that I may emphasize certain aspects.

"President Armstrong, a scholar in his own right, has had wide experience in scholarly activity and academic administration. He is cognizant of the problems which confront university presidents when a medical school is on campus. He seems eager to face the challenges if a substantial case for a medical school on the campus can be made. Inasmuch as the success of a university medical school is dependent upon the support of the president of the university, President Armstrong's attitude and ability is considered an important asset by the commission."

In their survey of Calgary hospitals the commission noted, in reference to the Foothills General Hospital, that the hospital, "While being built by the Provincial Government, has an appointed Board of Governors and a locally appointed Medical Advisory Board. There is a Nursing School adjacent to the hospital and the director of the school has been appointed and the school is in operation. A superintendent of the hospital has been appointed who is a layman and he will appoint a medical superintendent who will be his assistant. Although it is situated on a magnificent site, the hospital is across the Trans Canada Highway about a mile from the university."

"It is established that a medical school, that is to say the Faculty of Medicine of a university, can gain a great deal by close proximity to other university departments. This need for close working relationships applies not only to the basic medical departments, such as anatomy and physiology, but also to departments such as medicine, surgery, obstetrics, and psychiatry, which are necessarily located within the teaching hospital. It follows that the ideal relationship is one in which the main university's scientific departments, the pre-clinical medical departments, and the hospital are located on adjoining areas of the same site. In Calgary, we are assured that there would be no problem in providing a site for the pre-clinical medical departments immediately alongside the common science building."

"The relationship between the University and the governing body of its principal hospital is of great importance. It is our considered opinion that to insure recruitment of staff of suitable quality at all levels the University must have full control of all appointments. It is our considered opinion that in order to make it possible for teaching to be conducted in a satisfactory way the University must have full control over the conditions governing admission of patients. We are of the opinion that the most satisfactory solution would be to build a University Hospital, of say 350-400 beds, on the ideal site envisioned above. This plan of a combined medical school and teaching hospital related to the general science building on the university campus would give Calgary an opportunity to establish a centre for medical teaching and progressive developments which would be second to none in the western world."

The report recorded the commission's interaction with other faculty members. "They did not view the medical school as a status symbol, nor did they fear the presence of basic medical sciences as a threat to their own programs. They obviously had been giving serious consideration to the question of a new medical school, and it was satisfying to note that they were prepared not only to cooperate but also to experiment in the areas of pre-medical and pre-clinical education."

In western society, it is becoming increasingly evident that medicine, while in its practice retaining some of the characteristics of an art, is rapidly more and more dependent upon the scientific method. In Calgary, those interviewed seemed to accept this fact and seemed willing to bend their efforts to make the physician not only well educated in the classical sense but knowledgeable in the basic physical, chemical, and behavioral sciences related to medicine.

The commission envisioned the Health Sciences Centre as one which would immediately plan to include a Faculty of Dentistry (an anticipated early need in the province, in their opinion), a Faculty of Nursing (in an active planning stage at the present), and to provide within the Health Sciences Centre arrangements for the training of various paramedical personnel such as Radiology Technicians, Laboratory medical workers, etc.

Kirchner: Now I would like you to proceed with your perceptions as to how these aims and recommendations were carried out and fulfilled.

McNeil: The committee was chosen for the purpose of selecting the Dean of Medicine. It consisted of Dr. W. Trost (Vice President Academic) as Chairman, and the members, Dr. Baker (Education), Dr. T. Penelhum (Arts), Dr. Neville (Engineering), Dr. Hyne (Chemistry and later graduate studies), Dr. Hartland Rowe (Science), and myself. The members of the committee, other than myself, were the most senior faculty at Calgary. It was unfortunate for the institution that the wise Dr. Trost did not remain at Calgary. The committee sought applications widely and the "short list" finally included three men.

Kirchner: Dr. W. Cochrane, of course, would be one, but who were the others?

McNeil: I am afraid that I now cannot remember their names. I could possibly obtain them from University Archives or from the Vice President's (Academic) office. They were all excellent men. Only one of the interviews is at all fresh in my mind, other than Dr. Cochrane's. This was the then Dean of Medicine at the University of Vermont, I think. We were most impressed with this man and he might well have been offered the position. We would have been bringing him in from an established school of medicine, and his qualifications were completely satisfactory. He gave us the distinct impression that his interest in coming to Calgary was not great. A salary of some forty-five thousand dollars a year would be an initial demand before he would consider making this great change in his life. This income now seems paltry, I'm sure you will agree. However this one stipulation was a major influence upon us and our decision not to invite him. I cannot remember that anyone took the time to show him any of the many attractions which Calgary and environs could offer. I think that I would have considered it, but I suppose I thought that I could not find the time to do this properly. I do know that something as important as this should have had a major priority.

Dr. Cochrane was, at the time, the head or in the Department of Pediatrics at Dalhousie in Halifax. He was obviously very keen from the outset to receive the invitation for the position. I remember one of my questions to him was, "Should the provincial government fail to carry out the recommendation of the commission as to building a University Hospital on campus, what would be your reaction?" His response, as I recall, was that this would not deter him from proceeding with the plans for the faculty, and he would use the Foothills Hospital as the University facility, notwithstanding its drawbacks as indicated in the commission report. I cannot remember the other questions but I do believe that the committee failed to uphold Dr. Armstrong's admonitions which the commission had so strongly supported. Had we done so we might have avoided some of the unhappy events which occurred later.

Kirchner: Who made the decision that the school would produce family physicians?

McNeil: The commission made recommendations with regard to general practitioners. These recommendations pertained to the availability of continuing education for practitioners in the southern half of the province. They acknowledged the work of Dr. Kling's department in Edmonton and stated that similar arrangements should be made within the Health Sciences Centre in Calgary. The Minister of Health, Dr. Donavon Ross (a general practitioner) had the opinion that the school at Calgary should have as a primary responsibility the training of general practitioners. Family Medicine was not a specific designation then, as I recall. I have always thought that such a recommendation was rather naive in that it would be difficult to restrain a physician in his desire to become further trained and become competent in a particular area of medicine.

Kirchner: Exactly when was it that Dr. Cochrane was appointed Dean of Medicine?

McNeil: I would think it was within the year 1967.

Kirchner: You mentioned that even the Alberta Dental Association was asked and provided a very positive, encouraging answer to the question of a medical school in Calgary. At the time, was it considered that a dental faculty would be added?

McNeil: The commission spent some time with the dental faculty in Edmonton. They were well aware of the situation of dentistry in the province. As I have said, they predicted the early need for a second dental school in Alberta, and recommended that the Health Sciences Centre should plan to incorporate this faculty. The dentists of Calgary, observing the development of the medical school, naturally made representation, so that they might see the recommendation for a dental school fulfilled. Dr. Armstrong appointed a committee, and again I was placed on this committee. One of the members and chairman I think was a Dr. Arai.

Kirchner: The biologist?

McNeil: Yes. There were one or two others on this committee but I particularly remember Dr. Arai. The committee made no positive recommendation in this regard. I did feel that the government had committed itself to health education about as much as it would do so for the present. Perhaps I could mention that at about this time the dentist, Dr. Gordon Swan, my friend and our family orthodontist, was made chairman of the Board of Governors of the University. He distinguished himself in this position and the Dr. Gordon Swan Mall on the campus is a recognition of his great contribution. Dr. Cochrane and he became close friends and a son of the Cochrane's married one of Gordon's and Margaret's beautiful daughters.

TWENTY FIVE

Kirchner: Will you perhaps proceed with the development of the Medical School as perceived from your vantage point?

McNeil: Dr. Cochrane produced a "Philosophy of the Calgary Health Sciences Centre". I cannot lay my hands on it at this time, but I recall being impressed with it. I was not part of the decision making process with regard to the further developments of the medical school. I was asked by two of the applicants for Heads of Department appointments to provide references for them. These positions were namely that of the Department of Surgery. Dr. Harry Brodie, one of my former interns at the Calgary General was one of these, and he subsequently became the Head of Gynecology and Obstetrics. Dr. Robert Pow was the other, but he was not successful in his bid for Chairmanship of the Department of Surgery.

The pre-medical academic requirements of the faculty were a new departure. There were almost no prerequisites and no recognizable calendar for such a course other than evidence of superior academic performance. I am speaking of that time only; no sciences, languages, or humanities were catalogued as necessary. I understood that a Physical Education degree could be taken as constituting a pre-medical course. The makeup of the membership of the selection committee for applicants to the school was a departure too, and was interesting and wise in some respects. Rather than being composed only of doctors, it was made to be made up of laymen (I am not sure whether nurses or other professionals were included) and possibly only one doctor. That a first year medical student be an essential member of this committee was a little too much for me. I saw one applicant who said that the only one who interviewed him was the medical student. The anatomy specimens were prepared for the students in part, at least, by University of Alberta students. No dissection exercises were required of the Calgary students. There were no pre-clinical years, as is generally understood. The course of three academic years was constructed on a "system" method and, as you know, there were no distinct pre-clinical subjects. A multi-discipline laboratory or space was provided in the Foothills Hospital, where I understand a cubicle of some type was made available to each student. I do not know whether any effort was ever made to associate the faculty with other university faculties like Arts

133

and Science as was envisioned by the commission. I do note that the commission did mention in their report that experimentation in "system" teaching had been tried elsewhere and that the Health Sciences Centre might possibly take this into consideration. I was a member of a committee for the selection of a Head of the Department of Family Medicine. The terms of reference of this committee stated that a successful applicant must have no other academic qualifications than his primary medical degree. Limited qualifications seemed unusual to me and I recall that Dr. Dawson (the Associate Dean), in answer to my question as to whether training in ophthalmology would disqualify one, I was told that this was so.

The student of the late sixties was quite a contrast of that of previous times and often openly rebellious. The broad outlook of the early selection committees brought examples of the extremes of this student attitude. Students might feel no responsibility to attend class and if he did he might, for example, turn his back upon the lecturer, or openly disagree with any and all statements made. The recourse mechanism provided for the student to voice any objections almost brought anarchy in my opinion. Dr. Brody, when he threatened to fail students who did not attend his teaching sessions, was told by students that he would be reported to the Grievance Arrangement (or whatever it was called). I have seen a guest lecturer dissolve in tears after a session with some of these self appointed "prima donnas". I believe that the twelve month sessions which prevents the opportunity for a student to separate himself from academia to experience other people and situations for a few months each year, was a backward step. Dr. Armstrong, whom the Commission acknowledged so strongly in reference to the medical school, resigned very early on. I do not think that this was related to differences with the medical school, but rather to the impossible situation he found himself in with the abrasive and pragmatic Chancellor of the university, the Chief Justice Campbell McLaurin. This was a distinct loss to the University of Calgary.

Kirchner: You have given a frank description of your observations and reactions to the very early history of the medical school. Perhaps now you will tell us your assessment of the early academic results and how they measured up to the initial visions of the school's creators?

McNeil: The first class, after difficult times (particularly for the faculty in adapting to this new curriculum), graduated in 1973. This was two years earlier than predicted by the commission. Two further years of experience were mandatory for licensure. The first convocation was held in the central hall of the new Health Sciences Building, entirely separate from the other faculties. The makeup of the platform party was interesting. Having in mind the role of the Alberta Medical Association and the College of Physicians and Surgeons in the creation of the school, neither were represented. The Foothills Hospital while not apparently first included, demanded representation in recognition of the fact that they provided the space for the faculty when they did not have a building of their own. The Dean had some difficulty administering the time honored Hippocratic Oath to the class, and obviated possible objection by the suggestion that the graduates accept the contents of the oath as they personally perceived it. The graduates of these classes evolved into confident and enthusiastic physicians who I believe performed admirably in national examinations such as the Dominion Councils. A number have excelled in the profession. I do not think that the General Practice goal was reached, but this has not succeeded elsewhere. The College of General Practice has been unable to foster a program that will produce a physician trained to meet the comprehensive requirements of the rural, more self-reliant, doctor.

When one reviews the recommendations of the Commission, one can observe the following: that the first recommendation was that of the appointment of the Dean; the second was that the school should be an integral faculty of the University of Calgary and this, one can say, did not result. The third was the reference to the inclusion of a dental faculty and the Faculty of Nursing and the facilities for the training of paramedical personnel in the centre; all of which failed to occur. The dental faculty has not evolved, and the Nursing Faculty exists entirely separately on the main university campus, (more in keeping with what the commission envisioned for all health education) and the fourth recommendation, pertaining to the separate hospital situated on the campus under the control of the University, did not come about. The recommendation that teaching units be established in the Holy Cross and General Hospital was realized.

The Dean and the Associate Dean resigned within a year or two after the first convocation. Dr. Cochrane went on to become deputy minister of health in the Government of Alberta (1973). Years later he became President of the University. After one term he resigned, again leaving academic life, to accept a senior position in the drug industry. The new Dean, Dr. Lionel McLeod, when asked some time later about the details of the creation of the medical faculty at Calgary, is reputed to have said that he had no idea at all of how it came about. A great number of highly qualified physicians and researchers have come to Calgary; the latter often bringing with them, or attracting large endowment funds, all to the benefit of Alberta. The Calgary physicians who became associated with the school have enjoyed the rewards that the medical college brought. My University appointment, although a full time board appointment, was not in the faculty of medicine. I employed some of the faculty in the Student Health Services and regularly provided patients and facilities for students. The past Dean of Medicine, Dr. Marvin Bala of Saskatchewan, was employed as an internist for a session or two at the Student Health Service. I might suggest references to this in Dr. Morris Gibson's (the head of Family Medicine) book, *One Man's Medicine*.

TWENTY SIX

Kirchner: What happened after 1970?

McNeil: I carried on my work as a preceptor for interns at the Holy Cross and the General Hospital. Some of these doctors should be mentioned: Dr. John Hantho, Dr. Paul Harris, Dr. Harry Brody the professor of Gynecology and Obstetrics — who died so prematurely, Dr. Jack Manes, and Dr. Beiber — the administrators of the Holy and General Hospitals, Dr. Morris Vernon, Dr. Stewart Cameron, Dr. Kent Remington, and Dr. Vince Murphy are a few who come to mind. I was one of the first to join the Foothills Hospital staff at a time before it opened and while it was developing some of its plans.

Kirchner: Did you continue as head of Internal Medicine at both hospitals?

McNeil: No. I was still Chief of Medicine at the Holy Cross until the late sixties.

Kirchner: Would you tell us something about the Cancer Clinic for I believe that you were associated with this program.

McNeil: The Cancer Clinics were founded in 1942 by the provincial government. The first Calgary Clinic with Dr. Jim Francis and later Dr. Tom Meilling directing it, was first situated in the basement of the Holy Cross, but was later moved to its own building next door to the same hospital. As you know, now it is a part of the Foothills Hospital complex and the old building on Second Street West is a general practice centre. The Cancer Clinics provided diagnostic services, but the only treatment offered at first was radiation therapy. The medical or surgical treatment recommended by the consultants was carried out by practicing physicians in the community. The consulting staff was also recruited from city doctors. No specifically qualified oncologist was available up until recent times. Dr. Edwin Smith and Dr. Priscilla Barnes were the radiologist and radiotherapist. The present radiotherapist is Dr. Barnes — Priscilla's spouse. The Cancer Clinics did not bring to the communities new expertise at first, but merely authorized and paid for the treatment recommended. However, the Clinics were considered authorities on these diseases. I was employed as a consultant in Internal Medicine two mornings a week for some years. My particular interest has always been hematology, and I did some of the first oncology in the city, being, I think the first to use many of the alkylating agents

137

(derived from nitrogen mustard) and drugs for Leukemia such as Aminopterin.

Kirchner: You mentioned that you also served on the HOPE, the hospital ship. How did this come about?

McNeil: For a long time, I had a desire to do something in the way of international health care. In an esoteric sense I suppose I had some notion of contributing to less fortunate countries; perhaps it was just seeking adventure! I made some effort to join other projects such as C.U.S.O. or Medico but these did not work out because of the time commitments and other things. We had at least two Calgary doctors who had previously served with HOPE. One was a skin specialist, Dr. Ben Fisher and another, Dr. Ernie Johnson, the ophthalmologist in town, who has made such a major contribution to Operation Eyesight. Dr. Johnson served with HOPE twice, and I think more than one term doing ophthalmological surgery for Operation Eyesight in India. I wrote to a Dr. Walsh, the founder of the HOPE concept. The ship was called the "HOPE" but the meaning of the organization is "Health Opportunities for People Everywhere". The HOPE now does not exist as a ship but still offers a unique medical education program for doctors and health workers in the country chosen. The HOPE health member works with a counterpart from the country visited. A health worker, a physician, a nurse or otherwise from the foreign country is matched with a "HOPE" doctor. The thrust of the programs is education not service. Following much correspondence I was eventually appointed the Chief of Medicine on the ship for a period of three months. The ship was then based in the harbour at Tunis, Tunisia. Mary Lou busied herself in preparation for her part, by retraining at the Holy Cross to update her A.A.R.N. The ship itself was a refurbished U.S. Hospital ship which had been in operation during the Korean War.

Kirchner: Did you get paid?

McNeil: No. It was quite a contribution as I think about it. We had four children and we were away for a considerable time. My flight and travelling expenses were paid for but this did not include Mary Lou. Mary Lou did her nursing in the operating room area (such work being her forte before marriage). She was wonderfully successful and received demonstrable praise for her work. She has several momentoes which were presented to her towards the conclusion of our rotation. The physician staff rotated for a three month period, while many other of the staff including nurses remained with the ship for a whole year.

Kirchner: That was in 1970?

McNeil: About 1970. I do not view my rotation as being as successful as I would have wished. As approximately half our time was spent on shore in the local hospitals, I was pleased with the quality of the relationships that I developed with the Arab doctors. Some of these men had received excellent training in notable French medical schools. They naturally felt they deserved a certain respect for their abilities, and they were not naive about the magnitude of the health problems in their country. My medical colleagues on the ship were, without exception, superior professionals. Several of these were Canadians including such men as Dr. Dobell who had performed the first Canadian heart transplant, I believe. It was rewarding to work with all these men and women. The nurses and other staff members were of the same high caliber. The plastic surgery done was remarkable and the skin grafting which was taught would be most valuable to the people there. Great disabling burn scars resulted from accidents common in Tunisia, where children did the family cooking on mobile burners on the street. While having the opportunity to see the exotic diseases which occur in these areas I would like to emphasize that it was the common scourges of the world such as tuberculosis, venereal disease, rheumatic fever, trauma, and genetic disease which occupied our time. My problem arose primarily from my deficiencies in the language. I could interact with my resident, a Dr. Hentatti, quite well as he could speak some English, but I could not function fluently enough to converse with young medical students whose first language was Arabic and the second almost always French.

We did have wonderful experiences, however. Mary Lou had kept a diary, and to recite all of the events would not be possible now. We were able to travel around much of North Africa from the Sahara to the Mediterranean, from oasis to Arab cities, from cave dwellers to cliff dwellers, to view the remains of ancient Carthage and the ruins of Roman cities such as Dugga to the battlefields and cemeteries (of both sides) of the last war. We concluded that trip with a holiday in lovely Majorca and after that a visit with relatives in England.

When I returned in 1972 I carried on my practice at the Calgary Associate Clinic. I had tried to divest myself of the University work as I have told you before. Dr. Armstrong and Charles Linton (the student affairs officer) made a plea to entice me to accept a University fully tenured appointment.

I was assured that I would not have to surrender my consulting practice entirely but would be free to devote a portion of my time to this and also that the University would look after my professional business and office requirements and that the security of pension, benefits, etc. would be mine. After much thought and deliberation I eventually resigned from the Associate Clinic.

Kirchner: I believe you have told us that you did not have an appointment to the Medical Faculty?

McNeil: That is correct. I would have been complimented had some arrangement such as a joint appointment been offered. I suppose that had I requested such it would have been granted.

Kirchner: How long did you continue as Director of Health Services?

McNeil: Until 1979. I had reached University retirement age by then. The dislocation from much of the medical life I knew when I joined the University was a sacrifice. I would like to tell you of one of the major rewards that I did receive. I was entitled to a sabbatical leave as is available to faculty. I was encouraged to take such an opportunity and this encouragement came in particular from Dr. Bill Cochrane, now president of the University of Calgary. I did have a plan for the study I would accomplish during this period, and this, briefly, would be to encompass a view, first hand, of University Health Services around the Pacific Rim countries. As I dallied in preparing my thesis for my application, my great friend David Schonfield of the Department of Psychology (a renowned authority on the psychology of Aging) prepared the document for me. This application was promptly accepted and we made plans to travel. I had written to a number of health services in various countries, seeking the privilege of visiting them. These countries included the United States, Australia, New Zealand, and Hawaii. Our plans for travel were more extensive than just these countries. We left Alberta in August 1978 and by car visited a number of health services in the western and southern states. From our visit and residence at the Faculty Club at Berkeley in California, we embarked on a freighter, "The President McKinley" of the American President Lines. We sailed for Japan, Korea, and Hong Kong in September passing under the Golden Gate Bridge about midnight on a warm fall evening. We listened to the Grey Cup play by play in our large stateroom while in the mid-Pacific. The Captain and the officers of the ship rapidly became our good friends. Again, Mary Lou kept a diary of the trip which tells of our fascinating experiences which could not be retold in anything less than a story of book length. We had visited Japan before on a medical junket which included Hong Kong and Thailand. Now we had much more time available to explore these places. Korea was viewed from the port of Inchon and the city of Seoul. The country then, to me, had not recovered very much from the recent war. The view of these countries as seen from the sea is of course far more interesting than the one obtained when flying. The oriental harbors of Hong Kong or Singapore would be difficult to describe adequately. Oh, to have possessed a camcorder! We spent some time exploring Hong Kong before flying on to Taiwan. There, as we travelled around that country, some interesting things happened. A reward for some minor medical attention to an injured restaurant worker resulted in an escorted tour to all the museums and intriguing places in Taipei. We travelled without making transportation or lodging arrangements beforehand in any country, but always received every assistance to make our local or continuing plans in the country we were visiting at the time. We continued our journey travelling to the Philippines and then on to Malaysia. In Kuala Lumpur, following a casual exchange of words, we became the guests of an English resident. His beautiful home, situated in a splendid residential district called Kenny Hill, was surrounded by lush vegetation. We then had the availability of his "Amah" or maid. She escorted us by car everywhere we wished to go. We visited the lovely island of Penang and then traveled south by bus throughout the length of Malaysia, stopping in places like the ancient city of Malacca on our way to Singapore. After an extended visit in Singapore, the wonderful country I will not attempt to describe now, we boarded "The President Roosevelt", another freighter of the same line we had travelled with previously. We were on our way to Djakarta but as we boarded the boat almost two hundred men, women, and children (many under five years of age) disembarked. Others had died on board previously, we were told. I will not forget the frightened, wild expressions of these Vietnamese boat people who had been rescued from a sinking boat somewhere in the China Sea. Crossing the equator and entering Indonesia brought new vistas. The steward on the ship demonstrated his concern about Mary Lou going into this tropical fleshpot of Djakarta and did everything he could think of to make things safe such as giving her various sprays, etc.; he didn't seem to have any concern for me! In Djakarta we visited the large general hospital where a patient of mine, a diabetic boy I knew while travelling there the previous year, running short of insulin had passed into a state of diabetic coma, and had been admitted there. His condition was thought to result from the use of illicit drugs and his medical care was provided very late. He developed a lower nephron Nephrosis and required renal dialysis to save his life. I had been in touch with the doctors in Djakarta from Calgary during this illness many times. I took the opportunity to visit these doctors and learn something about the life and work in this former Dutch colony. Next, we went on to Jogjakarta where the university is situated, as well as many artistic facilities and the ancient Boroburdier Temple. After this it was Bali, and of our travels around that island, rather than try to tell about that in a few words, I will say that on the beach I met the first topless girl (not Balinese — Australian).

It was a long flight to Sydney, Australia as we could not go directly to any northern Australian city. In Australia I resumed my visits to University Health Services. These were situated in the cities of Sydney, Melbourne, Canberra, Adelaide, and Brisbane. We stayed in student residences, sometimes in separate rooms and dined using the student's facilities. While we expected to be unknown in this country, we were wonderfully surprised to be met at airports and to be invited into the homes of health service staff. We had forgotten that we had been hospitable to Australian visitors to the University of Calgary. One director, having arranged a tour of the campus by one of his juniors, picked us up later and proceeded to bring us to his home. He reminded us of the fact that we had taken him home in Calgary, housed him, and further, that Mary Lou had done his laundry. We barely remembered his visit; thoughtfulness has its rewards. We did not get into the outback as one of the frequent airline strikes was in progress at the time. Remarkably, we did enjoy the same kind of reception throughout New Zealand. We travelled that country by bus and air from the north end of the North Island to the south end of the South Island. We continued to Fiji and on to Hawaii where I visited the last university of the trip. We attended a Christmas program at a girl's school situated on Mount Haleakala on Maui with old friends and patients of mine. We were met by Maunders and others of our family in December at Los Angeles airport.

While with the University Health Department, I became a member of and later president of The Canadian College Health Association and this required considerable travel around Canada. While in no way could it be recognized that I am a speaker, I have completed a number of papers and studies, some of which have been published. I might mention too, that while with the Health Service, I accepted an invitation to give an address at a World College Health Association meeting in Mexico City. I had the opportunity of meeting and talking with Mexican medical students. These "fun" guys laughed the loudest when a slide appeared (someone inserted it without my knowledge) showing a dinosaur among my most serious illustrations. My subject, I think, dealt with experiences in and the provision of college health services in Canada.

TWENTY SEVEN

McNeil: As I near the end of this long story, I cannot help but think of what happened to the Health Service after my retirement. My replacement was allowed to leave following his first year. The medical school assumed direction of it then, but the facility did not seem important enough to receive much attention. For example the infirmary did not warrant physician attendance, and the nurses have carried on as best as they could without physician support.

I have been a medical practitioner in Calgary for more than forty years. Over this long period it is natural that I should have shared many experiences. I have had many rewards and some of these have been professional and some personal. Recently, I was made an honorary life member of the General Hospital staff, a recommendation made first by the hospital board, not the medical staff. I am an honorary member of the staff at the Holy Cross. I resigned my appointment at the Foothills Hospital when I reached the age of 70. I am the recipient of the Award of Merit of the College of Physicians and Surgeons of Alberta, an honor which is only rarely made. I am an Honorary Life Member of the Canadian Medical Association.

As a physician the following is a tangible reward. A lady called me recently who had been a patient of mine for many years. She has been a diabetic most of her life. The medical supervision required the usual careful attention over the years. Pregnancy always provided new dimensions in management for both the mother and child. In our conversation she reminded me of my medical care, and spoke of the fact that I was present during the actual birth for each of the three children. She wanted me to know that her first boy's name can be found with the list of the most senior partners of a prestigious law firm in Calgary. Her girl is an astrophysicist; and her last boy is the senior environmentalist with a large petroleum exploration company in Alberta. She further said that she would like me to have a copy of her recently published book dealing with the wildflowers of Alberta. With the family, Mrs. McNeil and I shared many things, including sports such as skiing and curling in the winter, and water activities in the summer. Much of this was made possible by our cottage on the shore of Lake Windermere. I might acknowledge that the initial cost of the cottage was borne out of a small legacy I received. This legacy

Windermere Cottage, ca 1965. Dr. McNeil is at the right wearing a hat.

was the entire estate of a patient of mine. This lady, Miss Justine Bollman, a refugee from Lithuania, had been employed as a domestic all of her life in Canada. Mary Lou remains a beautiful woman, healthy and happy, and we have four children. My oldest daughter, Susan, (the one I did not meet until she was almost two years old) is married and lives on Vancouver Island. Prior to marriage, she was a qualified Dental Assistant, something to which she may return to when her two fine children Jason and Leanne are older. Their great avocation is the sailing of a grand seaworthy boat; I think this interest might have been fostered by Windermere. Marilyn, our second girl, demonstrated considerable athletic and academic interest and ability. She established track records here in the city and the attainment of one goal after another continues to consume her. She attended university here and obtained her Physical Education degree. After a period on staff at McGill University, she returned to Calgary as the basketball coach at U. of C. After winning the Coach of The Year award for Canada, she accepted a similar position at one of the Universities in California. She obtained her Master's degree, and has now almost completed her Ph.D. She manages a home and we all pride ourselves in her children, Tasha and Derek. Donald has followed my footsteps going into medicine. He graduated from Alberta, did his senior internship in Auckland, New Zealand. He returned from New Zealand by sailing ship travelling halfway around the world. His residency was taken in Montreal, where his interest in immunology brought him into contact with the notable Dr. Gold (cardio embryonic antigen) who is now the Dean of Medicine at McGill. Some further residency at the Foothills was followed by a period of successful consulting practice in Calgary. Not content with that he moved to the research department at the Scripps Institute in La Jolla. He now has a research unit and a faculty appointment at The University of Ohio in Columbus. His two fine little boys are Bradley and Graham. My youngest daughter Laurie wanted to follow medicine, too, but this she did not confess for some years. She was unwilling apparently to, in any manner, detract from her brother Don's enviable plans. She completed a medically related course in Occupational Therapy and did excel in this important work. She was not satisfied with this, however, and completed her Bachelor's degree and then her Master's degree in Education. She still relates closely to medicine, having married a doctor, and they have settled in Cranbrook, B.C. She somehow looks after a home, mothers Carlie (second name Lauchlin), Lisa and Christopher, while fulfilling an appointment with the Community College at Cranbrook in charge of international students; and these are only some of her activities. She tells me she is President of the University Women's Club in Cranbrook (which I think she founded).

THE DON MCNEIL FAMILY
Laurie, Don Jr., Susan, Marilyn, Don, Mary Lou.

Kirchner: Dr. McNeil, I should like to ask you, did you make special efforts to influence your son or any of your children in the vocations that they have chosen?

McNeil: It was Don's own choice. I or Mary Lou did not knowingly influence him or any of the children in their vocational choices. We must have, by some example or ethos influenced these ambitions (if one considers environment to provide the greatest influence). On the other hand they might have inherited their obviously ambitious personalities, as my brothers and I might have done, from my parents and in particular my mother. Mary Lou's parents were imbued with similar industry and ambitions for their children. Those years went by so very quickly and it is difficult to say how these influences came about. The telephone constantly rang at home over those years, and it would be difficult to imagine that this constant interruption impressed Don. We expected that they all would do their very best, as all parents do. We did the usual things such as attend the home and school meetings, visit the teachers, always taking distinct interest in all they were doing. Don decided early that he would enter medicine and this decision never changed. His enthusiasm has not altered and I can enjoy the opportunities I have to talk to him on subjects of mutual interest. I am complimented, as is Mary Lou, when all of the children turn to us indicating their regard and respect for our learning and experience.

Kirchner: Dr. McNeil, would you like to offer some advice to future generations of young doctors?

McNeil: I would indeed like to try to do this. I would initially state that they should not enter this profession unless they are prepared to make a lifetime commitment. They should follow the directives of the ancient Hippocrates in that they should truly consider their calling as the primary responsibility of their life. They must not expect to have all the privileges given to others, but realize that the illness of others has the first demand upon their hours. "Now if I keep this oath may I enjoy honor in my life and art . . . but if I transgress may the reverse be my lot." I would direct the student to Sir William Osler's *Aequanimitas* the content of which will be an excellent guide. To quote from *Aequanimitas*, (and speaking of the superior attitude which some embrace), "It cannot always be called pride, that master sin, but more often an attitude of mind which either leads to bigotry and prejudice or to such a vaunting conceit in the truths of one's own beliefs that there is no room for tolerance of ways which are not ours." I have quoted several times from a great admirer of Dr. Osler, my colleague Dr. Scarlett from *In Sickness and in Health*, and I believe that this book could sit in a place of honor on every medical student's desk. The code of ethics of the Canadian Medical Association provides a guide for the doctor in all aspects of his morality and responsibility. I believe, too, that the new ethical challenges will be met adequately by future directives emanating from such a body of physicians. The doctor's education must not be restricted to one medical school, one country, or even to one period of time, but must be a continuing exercise all of one's life.

I greatly appreciate, and am deeply honored by, the patience, courtesy, and the great amount of time that you gentlemen have granted me.